T0304516

ANTICIPATORY LEADERSHIP

HOW LEADERS CAN USE FUTURES THINKING INSIDE THEIR ORGANIZATIONS TO SHAPE THEIR STRUCTURES, CULTURES AND GOVERNANCE

ERIK KORSVIK ØSTERGAARD

ADVANCE PRAISE

"The 21st century is — and will become even more so — the millennium of paradoxes. Until now, we've had no 'field guide' for this.

Anticipatory Leadership is the guidebook all enterprise leaders need. It is practical and philosophical, focused and emergent, intellectual and soulful.

Full of wisdom and fueled by imagination, Erik's body of work doesn't just fill gaps that business schools, other books and academic research don't. It sets a whole new field in motion — one that all leaders need to become literate and fluent in, and capable of managing. Futures Thinking and Futures Literacy will become the core skills of our turbulent times in navigating an ever-increasingly paradoxical world.

Bravo, Erik, and bravo to all leaders who use this field guide for the future."

Perry Timms, Founder and Chief Energy Officer, People & Transformational HR Ltd, TEDx Speaker, Ranked Number 1 Most Influential HR Thinker in 2022

"In an era defined by constant change and uncertainty, business leaders face the pressing challenge of determining which internal transformations are necessary to maintain competitiveness. Organizations are increasingly expected to embrace diversity, establish purpose-driven roles and adopt sustainable practices. Simultaneously, they must revolutionize workplace methodologies in response to external changes, a growing preference for hybrid work models and the emergent integration of Generation AI technologies.

Anticipatory Leadership provides a methodology for utilizing Futures Thinking to engage in meaningful discussions about the numerous uncertainties and trends impacting the business landscape, and to effectively translate these insights into what needs to be changed inside the organizations. Erik illustrates these concepts through practical use cases and real-life examples, enhancing comprehension and applicability.

Anticipatory Leadership is an essential read for forward-thinking leaders eager to adapt their organizations to a rapidly evolving world."

Jens Jakob Svanholt, Associate Partner, EY

"In *Anticipatory Leadership*, you'll find a practical guide to embracing Applied Futures Thinking, as both a philosophy and a critical part of your organizational routine. This book offers tangible strategies and inspiring success stories, fueling optimism for those leading through the complexities of today's VUCA world. For forward-thinking leaders eager to stay ahead, this is an essential read."

Garry Ridge, Chairman Emeritus, WD-40 Company, and 'The Culture Coach'

"Erik Østergaard takes the reader on an inspiring journey through the practical application of Futures Thinking in his book *Anticipatory Leadership*. By dividing the narrative into four well-structured parts, he meticulously provides a framework for leaders to navigate and thrive in a chaotic world by identifying, organizing and using complex signals and trends to map a path forward, for both the individual leader and their organization.

Through solid research backed by practical cases, Østergaard makes a compelling case for why this book is indispensable for leaders eager to understand and implement Futures Thinking within their organizations. His insights help simplify complex concepts into actionable steps that can transform organizational culture and operational effectiveness on an overall and team level.

For leaders in Healthcare Informatics like me, Østergaard's strategies resonate deeply, offering personal enlightenment and professional guidance. This book has inspired me to reevaluate my thought processes and refine our approach to collaborative efforts, particularly in driving forward the future of digital healthcare. By applying the different tools, I've gained perspectives on how to better structure interactions with staff and clinical specialists to shape the evolving landscape of healthcare technology.

Anticipatory Leadership is not just a book but more a practical guide and an indispensable tool for any leader committed to ensuring a proactive and futuristic vision for their organization, large or small. It is especially beneficial for those looking to integrate Futures Thinking into everyday strategic planning and decision-making to be able to achieve comprehensive transformation."

Christian Koerner, Director of Digitalization at Rigshospitalet, the Danish National Hospital

"*Anticipatory Leadership* offers a refreshing, disruptive perspective on Futures Thinking anchored to practical application. Beyond theory, this book equips readers with concrete tools and case studies, enabling them to not only anticipate but actively shape multiple futures. Its focus on internal organizational environments presents a transformative approach that will unlock potential in navigating uncertainty and increase conviction about decisions of strategic direction.

Essential reading for leaders committed to driving meaningful change."

Richard Wood, Change and Transformation Consultant, Woody World of Work

"Who knows what's going to happen in the future? Can you even really be sure about tomorrow? Much like 'the butterfly effect,' things happen seemingly by chance that change what we need to do today.

Bringing order to the chaos of a changing world by identifying patterns and defining them and our relationship to these events — perceived, real or otherwise — is at the heart of Erik's concept of Anticipatory Leadership. He delves into a world of indefinites and possibilities, giving practical ways that we can bring some sense to the unknowns of the future.

In doing this, he draws from disciplines and experiences from across the practical, business and academic worlds, giving the reader structure and clarity in the murky world of Futures Thinking."

Charles Robinson, Head of Strategic Projects & Initiatives, Therapeutic Modalities, Roche

"You know you need something different. This is it.

Erik's book is for forward-thinking leaders who know that change management and transformation from within the organization are part of the solution to succeed in today's fascinating yet complex business environment.

By opening new paths, Erik offers a steady and grounded approach by both educating and guiding leaders to effective and pragmatic tools that can create big impact and positive effects on your business and employee engagement.

Most importantly, Erik brings refreshing perspectives on how to create a future where success is not only determined by context, but also by human agency. By diving into the required leadership and the emotional impact that Futures Thinking processes can have — hope, ownership, confidence and agency — Erik lays out a pathway where employees become an essential part of shaping and creating a future we all want to be part of.

He gives us a powerful guide to the practices now needed in business to become a 21st-century, future-fit organization, unlocking how both business and employees can thrive and co-exist together.

This is a book that is easily read and hard to put down."

Louise Raaschou, Head of Leadership Transformation and Strategy, Mercedes-Benz Vans Europe

"Embark on a journey of forward-thinking with Erik's groundbreaking exploration of Futures Literacy and its transformative power in the business landscape. In this illuminating book, Erik delves into the art of Futures Thinking, offering practical insights and strategies for harnessing its potential in strategic foresight. From navigating uncertain terrain to capitalizing on emerging opportunities, Erik's work is a beacon for building adaptable organizations. I am very excited about and looking forward to using it in our work, and ready to thrive in an ever-evolving world.

Discover how embracing and building Futures Literacy as a key leadership skill can revolutionize your approach to business, empowering you to shape tomorrow's success today.

Prepare to expand your horizons and embrace a new era of possibility with Erik as your guide."

Timm Urschinger, Transformation Architect, EY, and Co-Creator of Teal Around The World

"Imagine leading from the future, today. Østergaard delivers a compelling guide for leaders to shape their organizational future with clarity and confidence. Packed with bold ideas and smart, actionable strategies, this book equips leaders with the power to lead with foresight — identifying trends, embracing internal change and crafting strategies straight from the future."

Eric Solomon, Ph.D., Founder and CEO of The Human OS, Board Member, Speaker, Author, Coach

Published by
LID Publishing
An imprint of LID Business Media Ltd.
LABS House, 15-19 Bloomsbury Way,
London, WC1A 2TH, UK

info@lidpublishing.com
www.lidpublishing.com

A member of:

BPR
businesspublishersroundtable.com

© Erik Korsvik Østergaard, 2024
© LID Publishing Limited, 2024

Printed by Imak Ofset
ISBN: 978-1-915951-36-6
ISBN: 978-1-915951-37-3 (ebook)

Cover and page design: Caroline Li

ANTICIPATORY LEADERSHIP

HOW LEADERS CAN USE
FUTURES THINKING INSIDE
THEIR ORGANIZATIONS TO
SHAPE THEIR STRUCTURES,
CULTURES AND GOVERNANCE

**ERIK KORSVIK
ØSTERGAARD**

MADRID | MEXICO CITY | LONDON
BUENOS AIRES | BOGOTA | SHANGHAI

CONTENTS

ACKNOWLEDGMENTS

This book is the result of hundreds of conversations, workshops and action-learning activities with fellow futurists from academia, the private sector and the school of practitioners. I feel blessed and grateful to have met you and engaged with you in dialogues on exploring the alternative futures.

Morten Lindow at Roche, Kent Højlund at Pingala, and Evy Ottesen, Mette Husum and Frederik Persson at Steno Diabetes Centre Copenhagen. THANK YOU ALL for participating so engagingly and for sharing your stories to inspire us all.

Eric Solomon, Magali Musarella, Jeff Jensen, Else Marie Agger Hansen, Travis Marsh and Kasper Risbjerg, for sharing your observations regarding the trends and signals you sense around you, from Asia, Europe and the US.

Carsten Beck and Lasse Jonasson from Copenhagen Institute for Futures Studies, for numerous discussions and dialogues on megatrends and applied Futures Thinking.

Loes Damhof and Alex Lambie, who I met at The Emergence Academy at Hawkwood Centre for Future Thinking. You made me see the futures differently, paying attention to emergence. I owe much of my understanding and curiosity to the two of you.

A heartfelt and special message of gratitude must be shared with Perry Timms, with Timm Urschinger and with Virginia Morris! Not only have you shared your signals with me, you have all cheered me on, and I enjoy our regular chats and check-ins that have occurred over the years.

And, naturally, Line Bloch, by wife and business partner, for support, for rubber-ducking, and for sharing the vision of a better business world with me.

PREFACE

This book is written for forward-thinking, progressive top-middle leaders in the driver's seat for shaping, designing and developing their organization.

Leaders who strongly want to embrace modern organizational structures, and who want to transform their organization from the inside, but lack a methodology, language and tools to do so.

Leaders who stay curious about trends in society and technology, and want to adapt their organization to those developments, but struggle to translate that to the inside of the organization.

Leaders who sense the internal trends and signals and see a need for creating local variations of how they design their business model, their structure, their culture and their governance.

Leaders who want to embrace change management and transformation projects with all this in mind.

This book is a follow-up to my two previous books.

In 2018 I published *The Responsive Leader*, a description of the leadership style, mindset, roles and behaviours of modern leadership.[1]

In 2020, *Teal Dots in an Orange World* was published, providing guidance on designing your organizational context to enable local progressive teams, or 'pockets,' inside a more traditional organization.[2]

Both books addressed the so-called VUCA world, an environment of volatility, uncertainty, complexity and ambiguity. The term the 'Future of Work' resonated through them both. This book will build on that, and is as such a continuation of my body of work. It will bring Futures Literacy, Futures Thinking and Strategic Foresight into play in the tactical world of organizational change management — on the inside of your organization.

Futures Thinking is the methodology of exploring and evaluating possible futures, to shape the present. The specific formulation of this varies across the sources, but the fundamental idea of 'Using the Future' is the same: to think about the future, so we can make better decisions today.

The domain of Futures Thinking has drawn increasing attention in the past half decade, initially in the military and geopolitical arenas, then in the strategy work for corporate organizations, and lately in the academic world.[3, 4] The majority of the practical applications relate to strategy and to an organization's interaction with its ecosystem of markets, clients and customers, competitors, governments and vendors — that is, the outside of an organization.

In this book I'll take the philosophies,
mechanisms and tools from the strategic world
of Futures Thinking and bend them inwards,
inside the organization.

I'll help you use Futures Thinking in your
organizational change management and
transformation approach.

It will build on the academic approaches of 'Anticipation-for-the-Future' and 'Anticipation-for-Emergence,' as described for example by Riel Miller, the head of Futures Literacy at UNESCO, and build on the business approach to Strategic Foresight.[5] But, it will be adapted to a tactical world, useful for organizational change management and change enablement.

I will show how scenarios and Signal Sorting can be used to explore and evaluate the different futures for the organization, how assumptions can be revealed, reframed and rethought, what Anticipatory Leadership is, and how 'Using the Future' helps leaders make decisions about the present. In other words, **how thinking about the future helps you with your tactical, transformational change management.**

It will help the leaders answer these four questions:

- How do I use my understanding of trends and signals in society and technology to design my organization, culture and governance?
- How do I look for signals inside my organization?
- How do I challenge and revisit our assumptions and myths, which we build our view of the future on?
- What kind of anticipatory leadership does it take to be futures literate inside my organization?

My aim is to help you to use Futures Thinking as a vehicle for shaping your organization by exploring and evaluating the possible, plausible and preferable futures inside your organization.

This will give you a methodology and a language for structured discussions and discoveries.

I'm confident this will enable you to shape your organization, so that you can create precisely that kind of modern organization that suits you.

Happy reading!

Erik Korsvik Østergaard

INTRODUCTION

This book is about how organizational transformations can benefit from Futures Thinking.

For decades, my interest has been in the Future of Work: The domain of ideas, philosophies, movements and trends within work, leadership, organizations, governance and cultures. When those elements get put in the context of an organization, New Ways of Working appear.

Increasingly over the years, leaders have been looking for ways to adapt their organization and their ways of working to the development of society and technology. They want to shape their organizational design and governance to fit both their employees and the internal interfaces to other business units, taking into account various external and internal forces.

These leaders share with me a feeling of increased speed and intensity around them, a somewhat worrying outlook on Artificial Intelligence (AI) and its impact on production, communication and trust, and a shift in management from vision-based to reality-based execution. At the same time, they sense a desire for a more fundamental shift toward humanity at work, slowing down to speed up, regenerative leadership, and doing good in life (not only doing well). They observe these shifts and changes around them, in society, in the technology domain, and inside their organization.

Something is moving and shifting. These leaders are distinctly aware of this, and want to embrace it in their tactical transformation inside their organizations. They are both pushed and pulled into action mode.

This has led me to investigate how Futures Thinking can be a vehicle for these transformations, inside the organization. How can imagining alternative scenarios for the organization, exploring how trends affect the way we work, and uncovering assumptions and myths enable us to shape the way we want to work? What leadership does it take, and what emotional impact does it have?

From the outside-in, what changes by using the Futures Thinking methodologies on the inside of the organization?

Traditionally, Futures Thinking is used to consider the effects of trends and signals on the strategic market and to imagine possible futures that the organization could or should be part of. Moving the Futures Thinking approach to the inside of the organization changes the time horizon, the scope, the ecosystem, the involved people, and the source of the signals and trends. We want to investigate this in detail.

From the inside-out, how can we take trends and signals into account when we investigate and describe the possible scenarios for our transformations inside our organization?

Futures Thinking offers a methodology to do all of this, and we want to investigate the approach when applied in transformations. Naturally, we are interested in the process, but also in the sources of the signals, the myths and assumptions that we uncover, the anticipatory leadership it requires, and the effect on our structures, cultures and governance. Special interest will be given to the emotional impact that this can create — namely hope, ownership and confidence, and the relationship to agency.

Throughout the book our focus is on the architectural phase of an organizational transformation. We define a transformation as a significant and intentional change in the structure, culture, governance, processes or strategies of an organization. We will focus on the understanding of what affects the transformation and how we can imagine and describe the transformation scenarios. We will examine the visionary and architectural phases, not the execution phases of such an organizational transformation. The emphasis is on change enablement, engagement and mobilization, not on execution.

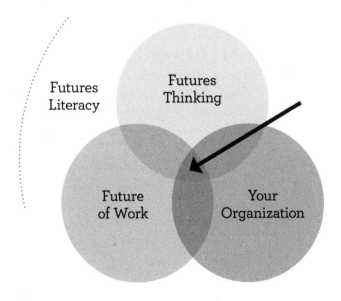

Figure 1
The Venn diagram of Futures Thinking,
the Future of Work and your organization

The book consists of four parts:

PART ONE describes the problem we are solving, the feelings of VUCA and BANI (brittle, anxious, nonlinear and incomprehensible), why Futures Thinking is sometimes seen as a disconnected methodology and what we can do to mitigate that, and the different approaches to exploring the future.

PART TWO introduces you to the central concepts: Using the Future, Futures Thinking and Futures Literacy. It presents the mechanisms and tools that are most relevant to the leaders who are designing, driving or supporting transformations inside an organization.

PART THREE applies the methodologies and concepts to the inside of the organization, combining and overlaying them with my 'Double L Double A Double E' approach. It also describes how to look for internal signals, and how the Anticipatory Assumptions play a role in the transformation. Finally, it helps you pinpoint the changes to the structures, culture and governance, as consequences of the transformation. Here we also introduce the Participatory Organization, describing the characteristics of a futures-ready organization.

PART FOUR describes the Anticipatory Leadership that it requires, the role of sensing, the emotional impact of Futures Thinking, and agency.

At the end of the book, you will find recommended sources for further reading, listening and watching.

A central element of Futures Thinking is trends and signals (internal and external), as they affect our work and how we design our transformations and change management efforts.

Throughout the book you will find reports from so-called Trend Receivers from the US, Europe and Asia Pacific, sharing what they see and sense inside the organizations they work in and with.

Every time you flip a page and find their reports, ask yourself:
- Will this phenomenon affect my organization?
- How likely is it to affect me personally?
- Do I like the effect of this phenomenon?
- Will my colleagues and employees like it?

The aim of these short reports is to inform you of what they see, and inspire you to look for those trends and signals yourself.

Scanning for internal signals is an integral part of Futures Thinking inside your organization.

TRENDS AND SIGNALS, SENSED AND RECEIVED BY PERRY TIMMS
Founder and Chief Energy Officer
at People & Transformational HR Ltd,
TEDx Speaker,
Ranked Number 1 Most Influential HR Thinker in 2022

Location: UK and Europe

- A more humanized way of working is emerging. "It's a duty to care for people." People First.

- Technology is overwhelming and immersive. "People are lost." Technology is solutions looking for problems.

- Pace is high.
  "It's too much, and too fast." It's both the tempo of production and of changes.

- It is not linear.
  "It requires looping and 'organizational parkour.'"

Timms reflects on what the morals of the future are going to be. At the same time, he's optimistic regarding climate change, the emergence of small, social communities, and a redesign of the economic models.

Note that some of the signals are directly counteracting and paradoxical.

PART ONE:

THE QUEST FOR CONTINUOUS ADAPTION

Let us start by understanding the problem we are trying to solve, and why Anticipatory Leadership is both requested and needed.

WHAT IS THE PROBLEM?

The following are a few quotes from the hundreds of conversations I've had over the past few years regarding the Future of Work, trends and organizational design:

"We need to change! We need to develop our business unit to fit with the megatrends, but we don't know where to start. We're too massive, too rigid to change, I think. And there are so many internal dependencies with the other business units and functions. It's so overwhelming to me."
— Senior Vice President in an international bank

"We cannot have just one monoculture and one homogeneous approach to our operating model anymore. We need to adapt to the local differences in business and engagement. I think we need to understand the nuances in how the global trends affect our local business, and we need to consider the local trends and signals. We cannot design that from HQ only."
— Vice President in a global life sciences organization

"I have this gut feeling that we frequently need to redesign how we collaborate — more frequently than we used to. And we need to be able to do it without having a massive corporate transformation program. We need to rebuild the governance so that we build for change. We should upskill our approach to restructuring such that it becomes an organizational habit."
— HR Business Partner in a global manufacturing company

Three patterns across all these conversations are:

1. An outspoken need for change and change-readiness.
2. A lack of certainty about the way forward.
3. An increase in the use of phrases like 'I think,' 'I feel' and 'I sense.'

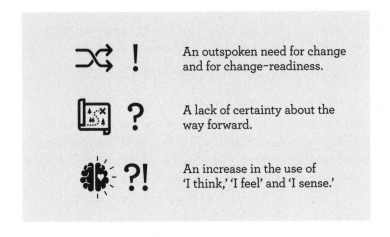

Figure 2
*Patterns across conversations with leaders about how they
perceive their situation and their challenges*

CHANGE IS HAPPENING
— WE NEED TO CHANGE

Let us investigate these patterns one by one.

⤭ ! An outspoken need for change
and for change-readiness.

The term VUCA was coined in the early 1990s by the US Army War College[6, 7] to describe a world that was volatile, uncertain, complex and ambiguous. People from academia, the public sector and the private sector have used it to describe a dizzying increase in pace and complexity. Those developments are not uniform across all aspects of life or in all regions of the world, but there's general agreement that advancements in technology, global infrastructural inter-connectedness, environmental challenges, the healthcare crises, geopolitical tensions and social media overload make the world seem overwhelming.

Since then, variants of VUCA have appeared. BANI (brittle, anxious, nonlinear and incomprehensible) was described by Jamais Cascio[8] from the Institute for the Future, in Palo Alto, California, in 2020 as an augmentation of VUCA. Where VUCA is descriptive of the present, BANI is future-oriented and dives into the emotional responses to these shifts in the world. I recommend reading the *Medium* article by Cascio before moving on, as he thoroughly describes the four aspects of BANI.

Taken together, these two acronyms nicely characterize the conversations and reports from the hundreds of leaders and practitioners I have spoken with:

The world is volatile, uncertain, complex, ambiguous.

The world feels brittle, anxious, nonlinear, incomprehensible.

The world is
VUCA

The world feels
BANI

Volatile

Uncertain

Complex

Ambiguous

Brittle

Anxious

Nonlinear

Incomprehensible

Figure 3
The notions of VUCA and BANI

From my experience, the leaders in these organizations register the VUCAness of their business world, and feel the BANIness, in themselves and in their peers and employees. It all means that they are becoming more aware of two challenges they need to handle:

One: Shaping their structures, cultures and governance to adapt to the shifting circumstances of their business and organization, considering local differences in cultures and operating models. This seems rather logical to the leaders in light of the conditions listed above, but it is also quite a formidable task. The change is transformational in character, and the number of actions required is almost unfathomable. To some extent this is not new. It is a continuation of a development we have seen for half a century, albeit unevenly distributed in where it affects and how hard. People continue to feel and talk about VUCA in their work.

Two: Tackling an increase in organizational anxiety about the future and engagement fatigue. The constant waves of change, the overwhelming heaps of daily work, and modern involvement-based decision-making processes make leaders and employees bow their heads, focus on their immediate, urgent tasks, and step back from engaging in discussions about strategy and the future. Adding to that, employees and leaders worry about the future, related to job security, having the skills for the future and 'getting onboard too late.'

> *"There is so much to do, and it makes me tired*
> *just to think about it."*
> —Middle manager in a Danish IT company.

So, what can we do? Here is the fundamental idea I will unpack in detail in the rest of the book:

Instead of looking at the whole of society, all the megatrends, and the full global organization and value chain, start by refining your ecosystem. Zero in on your 'circle of influence.'

Make your world smaller by looking at a part of your organization: the ecosystem inside your organization that you can affect.

Explore, evaluate, filter and sort the trends so that you work with those you find relevant, impactful and interesting.

Immerse yourself in future scenarios so you can establish a functional and emotional understanding of them, to help relieve your nagging anxiety about the future.

Uncover what you anticipate about the future and get a shared language with your peers, to help reframe your narratives and dismantle your false assumptions.

Use all this to make informed, better decisions about the change or transformation that you need and want.

The concrete way to do this is to use the capabilities and mechanisms from Futures Literacy and Futures Thinking, which are normally applied on the outside of the organization and apply them inside the organization. This will allow you to explore and evaluate the scenarios for your business unit. We apply these proven methods of Strategic Foresight only to a smaller scope, one that we can comprehend and oversee more easily.

Simply put:

We tame the VUCAness of our world by shrinking our ecosystem and exploring it in a structured way.

We thereby get acquainted with the BANIness of our emotional and cognitive response.

We apply Futures Thinking inside our organization, to explore and evaluate the possible and preferable scenarios of our transformation.

In that way we can adapt to the changes around us, and even affect the trends and signals to our benefit.

This is the idea that we unfold in the next parts of the book.

DO WE KNOW WHERE
WE ARE GOING?

Let us look at the second of the three patterns that emerged from my conversations with leaders.

  A lack of certainty about the way forward.

Roughly speaking, there are two variants of this that are relevant to us:

- Knowing the place you are going to, but not the path there. We must go from A to B, but we are uncertain about how to get there.
- Knowing the place you are leaving, but neither where you are going nor the way there. We know we are leaving A, but are uncertain about our destination and how to get there.

Going forward, I will be using this definition of an organizational transformation: A significant and intentional change in the structure, culture, governance, processes or strategies of an organization. Also, I will be categorizing transformations into two types, in alignment with the two variants we discussed above:

The Settlers Approach From A to B	The Explorers Approach From A to ?
We are Settlers. We know where we are. We know where we are going.	We are Explorers. We know where we are. We know we need/want to move.
"We are going THERE, and that's where we'll build our organization. Thus, we are colonizing the future state."	"We know we must move, but we decide our direction and destination based on what we discover. Thus, we are exploring the future state. We are decolonizing the future."
Symbolic act: Planting a flag.	Symbolic act: Looking through the telescope.
Useful when: Context has a high degree of predictability, and cannot be affected.	Useful when: Context has a high degree of turbulence, and can and should be affected.

Figure 4
Comparing Settlers with Explorers

Most of the change projects I have been part of in my 25 years of business have been of a third variant, namely *claiming* to know *both* A and B, *and* the road to get there. Getting approval and sponsorship from leadership is tremendously easier when you sound confident in knowing the problem, the solution, the application of the resources and the outcome. There are many instances of failed change projects. Stubbornness, lacking the courage to say, "I don't know," and failure to change your plan when you discover you're on the wrong track are some of the reasons why.

Across organizations, the nature of decision-making, the balance between predictability and adaptability, the culture, the operating model, the goals and much more may differ considerably. There can be different levels of volatility associated with external or internal changes. There will be varying degrees of hunger and curiosity for change. The context for your organizational transformation is vital for determining the approach, leading to either settling in or exploring the future state.

I will argue that both approaches to transformation can benefit from better understanding the future state before engaging. Thinking about the future state enables us to explore and evaluate both the design and direction, so that we can improve and adapt our approach, regardless of the type of transformation.

This is where the application of Futures Thinking really proves it worth on the inside of our organization.

Here's one way to define or describe Futures Thinking:

Futures Thinking is:
Using the future to make decisions about today.

Evaluating the future state, for either Settling or Exploring transformations, enables us to experience and understand the situation better. Traditionally, Futures Thinking — along with Futures Literacy and Strategic Foresight — entails terminology and approaches that are conceived as mechanisms on the outside of an organization, enabling it to adapt to the market, governments, customers and competitors. It uses global megatrends, developments and signals for scenarios, leading to updates in strategies and investments.

Here, we are investigating future states of **internal** changes and transformations. To do that, we apply the philosophies, mechanisms and tools of Futures Thinking internally, using both external and internal trends and signals. A new line of questions arises, which we'll unfold in the chapters ahead:

• How do I use my understanding of trends and signals in society and technology to design my organization, culture and governance?

• How do I look for signals inside my organization?

• How do I challenge and revisit assumptions and myths that we build our view of the future on?

• What kind of anticipatory leadership is required to be futures literate inside of my organization?

TRENDS AND SIGNALS, SENSED AND RECEIVED
BY MAGALI MUSARELLA
Strategy and Portfolio Manager,
Roche Pharma Research and Early Development

Location: France and Switzerland

- There is a management paradigm shift from vision to reality.
  - › There is an outspoken demand for leaders who can mobilize, communicate and connect people to strategy; leaders who are able to make decisions
  - › Team members value clarity and boundaries

- There is a call for diversity from within the organization.
  - › DEI (diversity, equity and inclusion) is not only put on the agenda from the top, it's demanded by the people in the organization
  - › At a minimum, diversity covers gender, ethnicity and cognitive skills

- There is a gap between a purely utilitarian vs. a 'meaningfulness' approach to work.
  - › There is a polarization between people who say, "It's just a job" and those who say, "It should be engaging and developing"
  - › The younger generation demands a need for purpose, growth, development and frequent change in their role
  - › You cannot expect people to be motivated just by the business, the industry domain or your company name

TRANSFORMATIONS IN THE FUTURE OF WORK DOMAIN

A significant aspect of any transformation is how you design your collaboration mechanisms: How the structures, cultures and governance look. This resides in the domain of the Future of Work, which when put into the context of the organization becomes your way of working. The challenges of change management and transformation design apply here too.

FROM A TO B, IN THE FUTURE OF WORK DOMAIN

Many organizations have been reevaluating their structures, cultures and governance in recent years. People are either inspired to do so, or pushed to do so.

Some leaders find inspiration from the professional literature, case studies they find online, conversations with colleagues or competitors, commentary by thought leaders or influencers, or scientific studies. They're curious about these movements and intrigued by how they can transform their organization. They immediately find energy and optimism in the prospect of that, and willingly start setting sail for the transformation.

On the other hand, some leaders do not have the pleasure of transforming based on willingness and interest. These leaders are forced or pushed to do so, in order to stay in business. They are losing pace when it comes to innovation or bringing products to market. Their competitive advantage is shrinking. They are too slow to make decisions. They have trouble attracting the right people and cannot retain their organizational role models. They're in desperate need of a solution to their problems. They must transform.

Both groups typically have two things in common: Their business justification, and their transformation approach.

The business justification is anchored in staying relevant to the market and staying relevant to their people. This is totally fair, and sound reasoning for transforming.

The transformation approach is largely the same for both groups: **We know where we are, and we find or design a new state that we want to transform into.** Regardless of their motivation — inspired or pushed; volunteered or 'voluntold' — the most common approach by far is a self-assured knowledge of the problem and certainty about the solution. We go from A to B, to stay relevant to the market or relevant to our people.

FROM A TO ?, IN THE FUTURE OF WORK DOMAIN

Over the past 3-4 decades, the development of modern organizational models has given birth to an overwhelming list of possible solutions, all of which are alternatives to existing operating models, organizational structures, decision-making regimes and cultures.

'New Ways of Working' movements like Teal, Agile, Holacracy and Sociocracy draw attention to them. Add paradigms like Lean Start-Up, Four-Day Work Week, Work from Home, Hybrid Work, Organizational Democracy, the Buurtzorg model, the Haier Group 'Rendanheyi' model, self-leadership, co-leadership, the unFIX model, Semco Style, SAFe ... and the list goes on.

There is an abundance of inputs and approaches, and the choices are many. I can fully understand that the list of potential solutions is overwhelming, and that leaders seek a simpler, leaner, easy-to-explain-to-stakeholders approach to identifying 'how to go from A to B,' and what B actually looks like.

Some people fall in love with a specific new solution, based on instinct or how the principles in the methodology align with their own mental model or mindset.

Some pick a solution based on who they hear it from — someone they trust, one who makes a compelling and convincing argument, a role model in their industry or a dominating thought leader.

ADMITTING THAT YOU DON'T KNOW IT ALL

These might absolutely be fruitful approaches that solve the problem and take the organization from A to B at the right pace. I have seen such transformations happen successfully, across various industries and organizations of different sizes, but it all relies on the premise that we know what we're doing and where we're going. It requires that the solution, direction and velocity are known and correct.

What if this premise is incorrect? What if the chosen solution or design is wrong, or the requirements for the end-stage change as we go along?

What if this sense that we know where we're going is a 'false truth,' based on our confirmation bias and an ill-conceived approach to coming up with strong solutions to business problems?

Harvard Business School leadership professor John Kotter suggested in 1995 that 70% of transformations fail.[9] Studies by McKinsey[10] and IBM[11] have revealed similarly dismal failure rates. Although this specific number has been challenged, there seems to be a general agreement that a substantial portion of transformations fail. The reasons are many, including but not limited to flawed solutions or failure to adapt to change. And so, the 'From A to B' approach might not be the right way, or deliver the right solution, in all cases.

How can you explore and evaluate the design and direction of a transformation initiative before you engage yourself and your organization in it? How can you apply Futures Thinking to understand your change and your transformation?

THE CHALLENGES OF APPLYING FUTURES THINKING INSIDE YOUR ORGANIZATION

Maybe you have tried it already: An offsite team day with your business unit. There's an inspirational talk about future trends, and a workshop on imagining the life and work in ten years. There's a nod to the idea that 'The best way to predict the future is to create it,' a notion variously attributed to the American President Abraham Lincoln or management guru Peter Drucker.

You draw detailed flow charts and role-play the future of work as you imagine it. In the end, a prize is given for the best breakthrough thinking, followed by a great dinner and entertainment. The following day, when you all get back to work, the emails have piled up, there are fresh fires to put out, and other than a fun shared experience, very little comes from it all.

I acknowledge that those sessions can work as one of several stimuli to get involved in Futures Literacy and Futures Thinking. But, I also question the long-lasting effect they have on the organization and the changes that are needed to become futures-ready or future-proof, however you might define that.

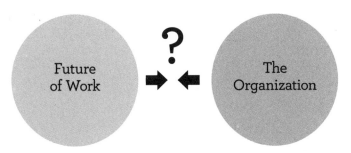

Figure 5
The challenge of contextualizing the Future of Work
with the organization

Applying Futures Thinking on the inside of your organization is not a commonly embraced idea. It has not been widely investigated or described in the relevant literature, and does not have a natural or intuitive place in the modus operandi of most organizations. There are various reasons for this, but let's look at the two challenges I hear of most often.

THE CHALLENGE OF 'SCALE OF MAGNITUDE'

Browse any airport magazine rack and you will find *HBR*, *Wired*, *The Monocle* and other business publications with similarly themed trend issues: 'The 25 technology trends that you need to embrace,' '10 shifts and shocks in organizations in the next 5 years,' or 'The 10 virtues of the future HR leader.' The same goes for publications, typically around New Year, from the Big 5 management consultancies, OECD, the World Economic Forum, or respected Futures Thinking groups like Copenhagen Institute for Futures Studies and Institute for the Future, or from academia.

Although these periodicals are well-known, well-researched and well-written, they all have the same relevancy challenge for the leaders **inside** the organization.

They address global megatrends — massive developments or disruptions in technology or society that are far beyond what leaders inside an organization need and want in order to transform their business unit.

First, the impact of the trends is on a different scale of magnitude, most often related to the market, customers, and how to adapt your products and delivery methods. That is, the impact outside of the organization itself.

Second, decisions on experimentation with or embracing those trends are typically also referred to as 'above my pay grade,' hinting that these discussions are expected to take place at the senior management level, with the board of directors, and as part of the strategy updates. The good thing about these publications is that they ARE very inspirational and DO work as a catalogue of understanding the world.

THE CHALLENGES OF 'I DID NOT ASK FOR OPTIONS, I ASKED FOR A PLAN'

This is also known as, 'Yes, I know I asked for input on the Future of Work, but what I was really looking for was an answer to our problems.'

OK, let's get the terminology sorted out first. 'Future of Work' is a concept of exploration and investigation of movements, trends and signals related to how organizations, leadership, culture, structure and governance at work are developing or might develop. It entails economic, sociological, technological, political and even philosophical questions and considerations. It transcends classical boundaries and is an interdisciplinary, multifaceted problem space that bleeds into many other relevant disciplines of abstraction.

'New Ways of Working' is a more concrete description of how collaboration, communication and coordination can take place. The prefix 'new' creates an intuitive opposition to how the current way of working plays out and alludes to a change or transformation from what is today. New Ways of Working is an umbrella term, covering specific methodologies like Scrum and Sociocracy, more principle-based approaches like Teal or Agile, and human-focused, bureaucracy-busting designs like Humanocracy.[12]

Leaders may ask for some input on the Future of Work, but what they really want is a specific solution to their near-term problems, which more resembles the methodologies of New Ways of Working. Referring to the earlier description of Settlers and Explorers, these leaders are prototypical examples of Settlers: "We know where we are, and we know where we want to go. Just take us there, please. Do not bother us with this Future of Work nonsense, which doesn't have an effect on us anyway."

Now, these challenges are very real, so how can we overcome them? Here's a proven approach:

1. First of all, **train yourself and your team in Futures Literacy and Futures Thinking**. Read that again. You cannot do this without strengthening your capabilities and getting accustomed to describing and reframing your assumptions and myths. Having a strong sense of personal consciousness and organizational consciousness in your team is vital. This is a team sport.
2. Make the **scope** of the application of Future of Work smaller, so the ecosystem you work with has a horizon you're familiar with, inside your organization. That can be your business unit or your network of teams. Context is king. Small is good.
3. Make the **timeframe** that you look at shorter. Five years typically seems to work.

4. Work with both **external and internal** signals and trends, so the forces and movements that affect you are relevant and sensible. This requires that you apply horizon scanning and look for signals and trends, inside the ecosystem we defined above.

5. Commit yourself to spend more time on **exploring and evaluating** the situation, signals and scenarios, rather than jumping comfortably to solutions. Get familiar with the possible discomfort of speculation.

6. **Involve colleagues and stakeholders** in your exploration efforts, getting their input and support.

7. Take all the methods, thinking patterns, tools and processes from Futures Thinking — which normally are applied with a longer timeframe and in a broader context on the outside of the organization — and **flip them inwards on your transformation and change management efforts**. You do not need to invent new mechanisms or tools. The existing ones are great; just use them on your ecosystem you defined above.

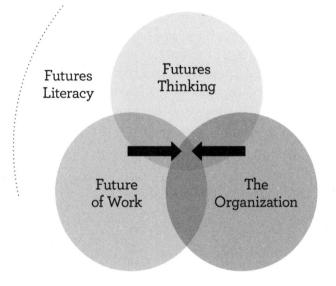

Overcoming the challenges of applying Futures Thinking

Futures Literacy

Futures Thinking

Future of Work

The Organization

Figure 6
Using Futures Thinking as a catalyst vehicle for bringing
the Future of Work into the context of the organization

- Get familiar with Futures Literacy and Futures Thinking as concepts. Acquire the needed theoretical knowledge.
- Narrow your scope so that it fits with the ecosystem you're in, that you can have an overview of, and that you can affect.
- Shorten your timeframe to typically five years, focusing on tactical changes rather than strategy.
- Scan the horizon of your ecosystem for trends and signals, inside your organization.
- Explore and evaluate the scenarios rather than planning for change too soon.
- Involve your colleagues and stakeholders.
- Apply the tools from Futures Thinking on your ecosystem, for your transformation and change management efforts.

In this way, Futures Thinking becomes the catalyst vehicle that makes the two circles intersect — where the Future of Work gets put into the context of inside the organization. Consequently, New Ways of Working similarly gets contextualized with the input from the internal signals and trends, and with the boundaries of the ecosystem and timeframe.

Is this the **only** way to do it? No. Does it work? Yes. When these three circles intersect, tons of relevant experiences, learning and ideas emerge. This is what this book is about.

REFLECTIONS FROM PART ONE

What kind of situation and transformation are you in?

How might we explore the futures?

How might we settle into the futures?

In both cases you can benefit from the framework and philosophies of Using the Future. That is, mastering Futures Literacy and applying Futures Thinking, to explore your futures or explore your roads to get there, or both.

This supports you in sensing unspoken and tacit movements, scanning for signals and trends that are affecting you, imagining possible futures, playing with them — and evaluating them, vocalizing the preferrable futures and storytelling about them — to make better decisions about today.

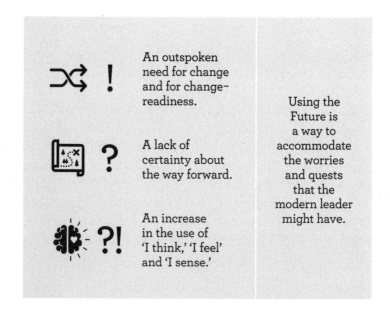

An outspoken need for change and for change-readiness.

A lack of certainty about the way forward.

An increase in the use of 'I think,' 'I feel' and 'I sense.'

Using the Future is a way to accommodate the worries and quests that the modern leader might have.

You might want to reflect on questions like:

How VUCA is your world? On a scale from 1 (strongly disagree) to 5 (strongly agree):	How BANI does it feel? On a scale from 1 (strongly disagree) to 5 (strongly agree):
Volatile: I feel that changes in my work and ecosystem happen fast, often and unpredictably.	Brittle: I feel that the systems and structures in my work ecosystem are fragile, and prone to breaking under stress.
1 2 3 4 5	1 2 3 4 5
Uncertain: I often find it difficult to predict outcomes in my work.	Anxious: I frequently feel overwhelmed by the amount of information and the pace of change in my work, leading to anxiety.
1 2 3 4 5	1 2 3 4 5
Complex: I experience numerous interconnected variables that make decision-making and delivery overly complicated.	Nonlinear: I've noticed that small disturbances can have big, unpredictable effects in my work environment.
1 2 3 4 5	1 2 3 4 5
Ambiguous: I frequently face situations where information is foggy, unclear or confusing, making it difficult to fully understand issues and hard to make clear choices.	Incomprehensible: I find many aspects of my work to be beyond my understanding, despite efforts to make sense of them.
1 2 3 4 5	1 2 3 4 5

Using the Future is a way to accommodate the worries and quests that the modern leader might have. This can include: acknowledging the need for change; stimulating change-readiness in the organization via participation, imagination and storytelling; mitigating and dampening the lack of certainty about where to go and ways to get there; tapping into the increasing outspokenness of 'I think, I feel, I sense.'

This leads to the four questions I want to answer over the course of this book:

- How do I use my understanding of trends and signals in society and technology to design my organization, culture and governance?
- How do I look for signals inside the organization?
- How do I challenge and revisit our assumptions and myths, upon which we build our view of the future?
- What kind of anticipatory leadership does it take to be futures literate inside my organization?

SUMMARY

Understanding the problem. The chapter begins with quotes from conversations with leaders, highlighting a need for change, uncertainty about the way forward, and an increase in phrases like 'I think' or 'I feel' or 'I sense.'

VUCA and BANI. Those leaders describe the world as VUCA and BANI to capture the challenges faced in today's fast-paced, unsettled environment. The world is VUCA. The world feels BANI.

Challenges faced. Two main challenges are identified: shaping organizations to adapt to shifting circumstances, and dealing with organizational anxiety about the future and engagement fatigue.

Two types of transformation. Transformations are categorized as Settling (when you know where you are and where you are going) and Exploring (when you know you need to move, but don't know the destination). Both benefit from understanding the future state using Futures Literacy and Futures Thinking. The challenges of applying Futures Thinking inside organizations are discussed, and an approach to overcome these challenges is presented.

The approach to be unpacked in the next chapters. The proposed approach is to start by: making the ecosystem smaller, focusing on a specific part of the organization; making the timeframe shorter; filtering relevant trends; exploring future scenarios; uncovering assumptions; using this knowledge to make informed decisions about change or transformation.

CASE STUDY: USING FUTURES THINKING TO IMAGINE, DESIGN AND DRIVE THE RNAHUB AT ROCHE IN BASEL, SWITZERLAND

Who
F. Hoffmann-La Roche AG (commonly known as Roche), founded in 1896 and headquartered in Switzerland, with more than 101,000 employees globally, is one of the largest life sciences organizations.

Their focus is on pharmaceuticals and diagnostics, among other areas related to cancer, the immune system, viruses, vision care and the central nervous system.

Elements from 'Using the Future'
- Standing in the Future
- Impact Stories from the Future
- Futurecasting
- Backcasting and Forecasting, for plans, structure, culture and governance
- Sensing and sense-making
- Internal signals
- Assumptions and myths

Approach
To help the reader understand the name of the RNAHub: In our bodies, diseases are often caused by proteins that are not functioning correctly. These proteins are produced according to instructions (like a recipe) found in our DNA. The DNA's instructions are copied into RNA, which then

helps make the proteins. Traditional medicines usually target these proteins. A new idea is to focus on targeting the RNA (the recipe) instead of the protein (the final product). This is done using nucleic acid therapeutics, which are made of the same building blocks as RNA and DNA. By targeting the RNA, these new medicines can intervene earlier in the disease process.

In 2022, the **RNAHub** was founded as a 'fully integrated multidisciplinary research community with direct access to all of Roche's current and future research capabilities' in Basel, Switzerland (https://www.roche.com/stories/rna-hub). Now, nearly two years later in 2024, the RNAHub consists of approximately 60 people in the inner community circle, and more than 200 employees in the ecosystem.

Several times during the ideation, design, execution and ongoing adjustment of the why, how, who, what and when of the RNAHub, approaches and elements from Using the Future were used.

From the very beginning, 'Standing in the Future' was used to describe so-called Impact Stories of the work taking place in the future. Impact Stories are a way to describe what you do, for whom and what it enables them to do. They are sentences, constructed like this:

In the future,
we <do this> so that <these people>
can <do this>.

These stories helped the core design team to imagine the plausible futures for the design and development of the RNA-Hub, enabling the team members and change catalysts to emotionally connect with the scenarios and to tell the stories of their intentions to the stakeholders in their ecosystem.

This, along with other strategic visualizations techniques, in turn supported them in formulating their 'Grand Challenges' as an aid for imagining, sensing and sense-making in relation to the future state they were working toward.

RNA Strategy Lead and member of the RNAHub, Morten Lindow, highlights one of these challenges: "Expanding [the] high predictivity, when it comes to pharmacology to all drug properties including safety, will be key to increasing both [the] therapeutic and innovation-enhancing potential [of the drugs]." (https://www.roche.com/stories/rna-hub)

Later, the whole inner community circle was involved in a Standing in the Future exercise, imagining the RNAHub five years into the future. By using a handful of storytelling frameworks, visions of both plausible and preferable futures emerged, with a diverse point-of-view on the science, the technologies, the data, the collaboration, the culture, the structures, the governance, and the people involved in the work-to-be.

This was followed by a Backcasting exercise, that resulted in a roadmap for the required artefacts and actions in that future, in two-and-a-half years before that, and back in the present. This kicked off a Forecasting exercise, showing the concrete projects and initiatives in their plan.

A fundamental outcome of this — and because of the inherent uncertainty of science — learning cycles was adapted rigorously into the governance and culture, reducing the planning horizon to a six-month iteration called 'Seasons' (like a series of episodes related to online movies). Similarly, the structure and the decision-making mechanisms were designed to fit the scenarios that they imagined during the Futurecasting sessions. These results and scenarios were revisited regularly at their so-called 'Pitstops,' where the inner community gathered to evaluate and adjust the scenarios and the forecasting.

As the RNAHub matured, organizational consciousness grew, and gradually they began sensing and sense-making of internal signals, organizational assumptions and cultural myths. For example, this could be related to allocation mechanisms, a focus on specific scientific or technological trends and advancements, or an apparent, albeit nonconfirmed, preference for execution and momentum. Some of these were embraced and included in the work; others were busted or deemed unlikely to affect the work.

Going into the fourth Season, the fourth six-month iteration, the RNAHub is once again planning to Use the Future to explore and evaluate the scenarios and the futures of their work.

Outcome and impact

As Morten Lindow reflects: "The outcome from the co-creation process seems to be significantly more valuable than the specific output from the workshops."

Confidence in the plan, ownership of the culture, psychological safety and belonging is on the list of emotional impact that Lindow highlights.

"Each RNAHub member, regardless of expertise, co-owns the success of the entire vision and all the challenges we need to overcome along the way," he smiles.
(https://www.roche.com/stories/rna-hub)

INTERLUDE: THE S IN FUTURES THINKING

This article first appeared in 'Futures of Work: Horizon Scanning Document 2023,' published that year by the Good Morning April organizational consultancy.[13]

There's one thing we need to talk about. This thing:

S

The s in 'Futures Thinking.' The plural s.

It is both attractive and repelling.

It is both intriguing and infuriating.

It is both a call to action and a decision-fatigue catalyst.

The plural S is there to underline that there are multiple futures to discuss, design and decide. Possible futures. Plausible futures. And preferrable futures. It also means that the specific and concrete future that we are going to experience is not destined yet and that we can affect it. The keyword here is 'can.' We can affect it. This is what both excites us and scares us. Yes, we can shape our future. But are we ready to take that responsibility, do we understand the consequences of that kind of freedom, and do we have the resources to make the changes?

There are circumstances that we cannot change nor affect. To name some, there are societal, geological, geographical, political, financial, physical, mental, habitual, cultural and national contexts that we cannot change. We all need to understand and acknowledge that. And we must investigate our own biases and privileges while we enter this realm of imagination and play with fantasy.

But the S!

On one hand, the S is a release of energy. The idea of exploring and evaluating possible futures is immensely flirtatious. What if ...? How might we ...? Who might be interested in ...? How is this going to unfold? Look at the massive amount of science fiction that is being produced and consumed. As a species, we're curious. And, we have the skill of imagination. The thinkers and scientists in this area call this 'anticipatory thinking.' We can imagine things before they happen AND create an emotional response to that mental image. We can describe and anticipate our next dinner. Our next vacation. Our next job. Our next place to live. Or maybe even our next 10 or 20 years. It is fascinating to play around with and to prepare yourself and your family for. Out of all these possible futures, some are very nice, attractive, and even preferable. We like those options. But some of these possibilities are unpleasant and unpreferable. Just think about the possible futures of climate change, to jump to one megatrend that is both immensely urgent to address and dystopic to imagine.

On the other hand, the 'S' is a yoke. With insight comes responsibility and the option to act. By using the mechanisms and tools of Futures Thinking, a range of possible, plausible and preferable futures emerge. And, logically, also insight into which futures we find unpreferable. This can be overwhelming. The S stresses that we must actively make some choices. We must explore and evaluate. We must say yes and no. We must overcome decision-fatigue, and act. Futures Thinking gives us a framework to have qualified discussions about the likelihood of events, and the likeability of effects. It helps us distinguish between the options and makes it easier for us to vocalize our investment of time, money and attention into either supporting a future or suppressing a future.

I am both an optimist and a possibilist. Naïve at times, too. I admit that.

But I do believe that Futures Thinking is an eye-opening approach to discussing, designing and deciding our next steps, regarding work, life and our planet.

TRENDS AND SIGNALS, SENSED AND RECEIVED BY VIRGINIA MORRIS

Global Human Innovation & Regenerative Futures Strategist, Founder of Bamboo Difference

Location: Asia Pacific

Signals:

- A stronger trust in intuition: Tapping into our inner voice of innate wisdom and knowing. More framing of discussions and decisions with 'I sense.' That's particularly important when limited experience or conflicting data exists.

- Shifting resilience to Buoyancy: A deep yearning to stay afloat without struggle. An ability to accept the constant waves of change with calm, courage and conviction.

- Playfulness: Approaching serious challenges with child-like curiosity and wonder. Connecting joyfully with colleagues and exploring solutions by learning as you go.

Trends:
- A more humanized work culture: A post-pandemic realization that we all bring our rich humanity to our working lives. A more vocal need to create authentic connections with colleagues and leaders, no matter the location.

- 'Success punishment' sentiment: As Asia continues to be the growth engine of global business, there are ever greater demands on this region to deliver higher results to cover shortfalls in other markets. This creates a feeling of unfair, relentless pressure to grow faster, just as when successful teams deliver great results so well that they are expected to deliver even more.

- Worth the commute: A higher expectation of what is gained by physically going to workspaces. A continued desire for flexibility and choice around where and how to work. An expectation that hybrid workspaces provide the opportunity to connect, share and learn, beyond just getting work done.

PART TWO:

WHAT ARE FUTURES THINKING AND FUTURES LITERACY?

This section of the book gives you an introduction to the principles, philosophies, methodologies and approaches to Futures Thinking.

I have chosen those mechanisms and tools that proved themselves useful for business application and beneficial inside organizations, based on years of applying Futures Thinking to projects, problems, strategic and tactical transformations, and operational change management challenges.

This is not meant to be a thorough or exhaustive description of the field. Instead, for beginners I recommend *Imaginable* by Jane McGonigal[14] and *Strategic Foresight* by Jan Oliver Schwarz.[15] For intermediate learners, *SCENARIO reports: Using the Future* by Copenhagen Institute for Future Studies is amazing.[16] For advanced learners I recommend *Transforming the Future: Anticipation in the 21st Century* by Riel Miller,[17] as it also embraces the academic approach. See this book's Endnotes and Recommended Reading for direction to further in-depth information.

In the pages ahead we'll cover those elements that are relevant and immediately applicable for the focus here: Using Futures Thinking inside the organization. This will be broad enough for you to get an overview and deep enough to provide an understanding of the field of Futures Thinking.

To get started, here are my rough-and-blunt descriptions of the two central components, Futures Literacy and Futures Thinking:

Futures Literacy is the ability and capacity to think critically and abstractly about the future. Key building blocks are the understanding of anticipation and assumptions.

Futures Thinking is the creative and investigative process of exploring and evaluating what affects us, to describe scenarios for the futures (in plural).

Note that the definitions of these two components are somewhat overlapping. A strict distinction is not always possible or needed when it comes to the tools and mechanisms, as the learning traverses and bleeds between the two. Using the approach from Futures Literacy helps you master Futures Thinking, and vice versa. Regardless, I will use this split going forward, for simplicity and to smooth out the narrative.

USING THE FUTURE – A CONCEPT

The future does not exist.
This is one of the fundamental truths about Futures Thinking and Futures Literacy. Only the present moment exists. Not the past, not the future. The future only takes form as imagination, storytelling, expectations, anticipation and assumptions.

As such, this creates a wonderful, useful contradiction because this 'applied imagination' instantly enables the existence of multiple futures.

Futures do exist, albeit only in our minds.

Creating, discussing and evaluating those futures makes it possible for us to make decisions in the present. We use this ability to imagine our next vacation, and decide on a destination, timing, means of transportation, accommodations and who we want to share the experience with. We make all those decisions based on our anticipations and assumptions about the imagined future. The same goes for how we plan for dinner, what clothes to wear to a coffee date next Friday, what line of education we might pursue, where we want to live, and with whom. We're using our understanding and interpretation of the future to make decisions.

It is this ability and capacity that we want to train for, hone and shape, so that our organizations can build the functional muscle, shared language and literacy of 'Using the Future' in our change management, our strategic and tactical decisions, and for transformation design.

Using the Future applies to several areas in organizations:

- Planning of activities and optimization of how we spend our time, resources, money and attention
- Preparation for expected or unexpected events, establishing a contingency plan, and performing risk assessments and risk management
- Exploration of shifts and shocks that will disrupt the modus operandi, where novel actors and elements emerge

The first two of those areas are typical strategic activities, whereas the last one is not (yet). This is where Futures Thinking and Futures Literacy play a massive role, as vehicles for revolutionary changes and transformations in an ecosystem that is turbulent. The ability to have a structured approach to exploring and evaluating those future scenarios is an organizational lever for continuous adaptation in VUCA times and, as such, a means of remedy for the challenges described in the introduction.

A transcendental leap of mind appears when we embrace the notion of multiple futures or multiple scenarios for the development or direction of our situation, either as individuals, business units, nations, peoples or inhabitants of this planet. We can create stories of multiple different futures, and imagine being part of them. We can describe dystopian or utopian futures, some more likely than others, some more manageable than others, and some more preferable than others.

By doing that we explore those future scenarios, and we evaluate them. We are also uncovering our assumptions, beliefs and biases. Assumptions about ourselves, our partners, the government and technology. Beliefs and myths about the political system, top management, strategic processes and how money is spent. We might uncover our biases as optimists, pessimists, longing for 'the good old times,' or preferring the status quo.

In turn, this leads us to make decisions in the present. We can choose to do nothing, or to act. But we have the choice. This is 'Using the Future.'

Using the Future:
To explore and evaluate future scenarios,
in order to make decisions today.

The idea of multiple futures was used increasingly in strategic thinking in the middle of the last century, where a shift appeared from a belief in predicting the optimal, positive future to 'embrace the quantum and organic worlds of open possibilities, chaos and complexity, and self-adaptive organization.'[18]

Especially in the 1960s and 1970s, researchers and futurists initiated a methodical effort to characterize the typology of the evolving futures approaches:

Futures studies approach	Futures types	Goals	Research methods
Critical/ postmodern	Preferred futures	Normativity emancipation	Text analysis, media critique, cultural educational artefacts
Cultural/ interpretive	Possible future	Alternative practical models, 'other' futures	Imagination, creativity, qualitative dialogue, ethnographic research
Participatory/ prospective	Prospective futures	Empowerment, transformation	Collaborative visioning, action research, activism
Integral/ holistic	Integral futures	Global justice	Integral, mixed methods, transdisciplinary, complex bricolage

This table is ©2010, Jennifer M. Gidley

The table on the previous page shows the different futures approaches, as described by psychologist and futurist Jennifer M. Gidley, adapted to the context of this book.

She highlights the effects we want to obtain by Using the Future in an organizational context: participation, a discussion of preferred/possible/prospective futures, transformation, empowerment, imagination, creativity and others. Note that this foreshadows the notion of the Participatory Organization, which we will discuss in PART THREE and a half. We can also extract from these possibilities that **our approach must be multidisciplinary, and require us to juggle several approaches and concepts in our mind and mechanisms.**

STRATEGIC FORESIGHT

To many people, across the Futures Thinking community and in the private, public and governmental sectors, **Strategic Foresight is an intuitive and practical application of Futures Thinking**. It is often also the first introduction they have to the field.

Copenhagen Institute for Futures Studies describes Strategic Foresight as "a planning-oriented discipline related to futures studies and focused on informing and shaping strategic decision-making, guiding policy, or exploring new markets, products and services. Strategic Foresight combines methods from futures studies with those used in strategic management."[19]

One can similarly define Corporate Foresight as "(...) identifying, observing and interpreting factors that induce change, determining possible organization-specific implications, and triggering appropriate organizational responses. Corporate foresight involves multiple stakeholders and creates value through providing access to critical resources ahead of competition, preparing the organization for change, and permitting the organization to steer proactively toward a desired future."[20]

Mark Frauenfelder from Institute for the Future describes 'Five Key Principles for Crafting Engaging and Effective Forecasts.' He describes these as underpinning both of the definitions above, suggesting that we: Don't Try to Predict the Future. Ground Forecasts in Signals. Cut Out Everything That's Not Surprising. Set Audacious Visions. Anchor Forecasts in Plausibility.[21]

All three sources describe: (a) The intention and approach of Strategic Foresight; (b) Why many managers and leaders struggle with applying it to their work.

With intent we see that Strategic Foresight is used as a mechanism for strategic choices related to 'new markets, products and services.' It looks outside-in at global megatrends and signals to adapt and develop the strategic direction and the investment of the business, the organization, or even the nation. Strategic Foresight became well established in the last century, driven primarily by massive global corporations like Shell and the military, combining the needs and methods from strategic management, risk management and business development. The intention is to escape the 'faster horses' trap. That is, avoid performance planning and optimization, and enable disruptive transformations.[22]

Strategic Foresight and the required capacity are typically anchored with the corporate strategy function, as they drive the strategic process. One of the outcomes is to establish forecasts, making it possible to distribute your investment efforts (both human and financial capital) where the value creation outbalances the risk. A clear goal to many, and a desired artefact to produce, is the strategy for the next performance period, including a budget for investment and operation, who to hire, and 'where to play.'

Meanwhile, as to why management struggles with applying this, its application is alienated from their work, regardless of how fascinating and thrilling the domain is to them. The scope is too large, the timeframe too wide, megatrends are on a global rather than local scale, and the strategy is a hand-down from top leadership. This is one of my primary motivations for writing this book: To remove that alienation, and instead make the application useful and meaningful.

> Maybe we should start talking about
> tactical foresight instead.

The key is to focus on the mindset, the approach, and on making the ecosystem that we apply Futures Thinking in small enough for impact, relevancy and holistic understanding. This starts with understanding and mastering Strategic Foresight and Futures Literacy. Training in Strategic Foresight is key, as highlighted by the academic Jan Oliver Schwarz.[23]

WHAT IS FUTURES THINKING?

Parts of this introduction appeared in 'Futures of Work: Horizon Scanning Document 2023,' published that year by Good Morning April, and have been adapted to this context.[24]

Maybe the easiest way to describe Futures Thinking is to spell out the popular, the scientific and the practical definitions of what it is.

THE POPULAR ANSWER

Futures thinking is a way to predict or foresee what will happen.

I have been asked hundreds of times over the past decade about the future of 'something.' Typically, the question comes from people who are on the verge of a transition with a lot of moving parts, and they need to have some stepping-stones to feel safe on.

'What's the future of leadership?'

'What's the role of HR in the future?'

'What skills are required as an employee in the next decade?'

I fully understand why we all look for those pointers and predictions. We need certainty in a world of uncertainty. We need some clear answers to foggy questions. We need to lean on someone who seems to have a firm idea of where we're going.

The challenge is that not all futurists like giving such popular answers, as they inhibit our wiggle room, do not allow for hesitation, and rob us of our imagination.

Even if you give (or receive) such answers, remember that they are filled with bias from both parties. Maybe the answer comes from a white, middle-aged male engineer, from the Nordic business world, with his own set of ingrained biases. And maybe the recipient of the answer has a similar set of biases. These answers can absolutely be useful, but remember that they are given (and received) in a certain context, with a 'this is my world' bias.

Your mileage may vary. The answers, no matter how firmly delivered or clear and logical they seem, might not bear any resemblance to how things will play out in your ecosystem.

THE SCIENTIFIC ANSWER

Futures Thinking is the study of imagination and anticipation and how it influences our decision-making, based on the use of scenarios.

It is a strategic approach to exploring and critically considering future scenarios in order to define the most preferable ones for people and society.[25]

Related to that, and for a deliberate distinction, Futures Literacy is the study of Anticipatory Assumptions. It is intended to help us understand how we think about things that have not happened yet, paraphrased from *Transforming the Future*[26] and *Patterns of Anticipatory Assumptions*.[27]

This scientific field is emerging. As the complexity of our challenges and worlds increases, Futures Thinking is needed in schools, businesses, politics and across society. Several universities are investing in this area and collaborate on shedding light on different aspects.

Using the future for better decisions in the present starts with understanding how we assume things, how we anticipate things, in what contexts they happen, and for what purpose.

THE PRACTICAL ANSWER

Futures Thinking is a way to evaluate the trends and signals in your ecosystem to explore and evaluate the scenarios of what might happen, so that you can invest time and money in facilitating the future you wish for.

This is an approach that entails many methodologies and tools, with many thinkers and doers who contribute to the growing application of the field. We've mentioned Signal Sorting, trend spotting, scenario building and Backcasting. There are dozens of other tools that help us in exploring and evaluating possible futures, and emphasizing and nominating a future that we prefer.

This can happen as part of strategic planning in a business, where key opinion leaders want to investigate the possibilities and keep nurturing a multitude of potential business ideas. We may also see it as part of solving problems in a society. And, Futures Thinking can help keep the ambition and aspiration of an organization alive and dynamic, rather than focused on a single-threaded tactical execution, however relevant that might seem in some cases.

The popular answer	The scientific answer	The practical answer
Futures Thinking is	Futures Thinking is	Futures Thinking is
... a way to predict or foresee what will happen.	... the study of imagination and participation and how it influences our decision-making, based on the use of scenarios.	... a way to evaluate the trends and anomalies in your ecosystem to imagine and evaluate the scenarios of what might happen, so that you can invest time and money in the future you desire.

Simply stated, Futures Thinking is the creative and investigative process of exploring and evaluating what affects us, to describe scenarios for the futures.

Futures Thinking has three major components:

A. **Tools and mechanisms:** The methodology of discussing, describing, exploring and evaluating possible futures, to identify those that are preferable in our context.

B. **Trends and signals:** An overview of the things that affect us in the present (trends) and things that might affect us in the future (signals and anomalies). We can call that the Magic Dust of Futures Thinking.

C. **Anticipatory Leadership:** The mindset of the people and organization, embarking on this task of Futures Thinking.

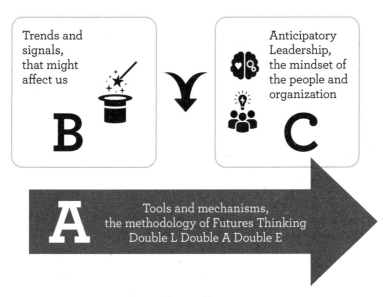

Figure 7
The three major components of Futures Thinking

TOOLS AND MECHANISMS OF FUTURES THINKING

The following is a collection of tools and mechanisms that are useful in a business setting, when applying Futures Thinking to your transformation and in your change management.

The overall process and approach are described at the end of this chapter, assembling it all into the approach called 'Double L Double A Double E.'

This chapter is influenced by books and training I've participated in, particularly the courses at Copenhagen Institute for Futures Studies, the Coursera courses by Institute for the Future, and The Emergence Academy at Hawkwood Centre for Future Thinking. (See Recommended Reading, Listening and Watching, later in the book, for further details.)

HOW FUTURES-READY ARE YOU?
Mapping Your Future Outlook

Investigating your outlook on the future can be done in several ways. A common pattern among the methodologies is to reflect on: your personal point of view on the predicted or perceived amount of change; how worried or optimistic you are regarding the future; how much agency or influence you think you have; what weighs you down from the past or present; or what attracts you about the future. Use these tools as a conversation starter and as a way to enable the participants to instantly get a feeling of each other's perspectives.

In *Imaginable*, researcher and game designer Jane McGonigal[28] suggests three questions, which I've personally used with success:

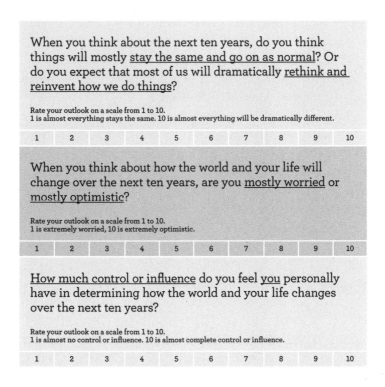

When you think about the next ten years, do you think things will mostly <u>stay the same and go on as normal</u>? Or do you expect that most of us will dramatically <u>rethink and reinvent how we do things</u>?

Rate your outlook on a scale from 1 to 10.
1 is almost everything stays the same. 10 is almost everything will be dramatically different.

| 1 | 2 | 3 | 4 | 5 | 6 | 7 | 8 | 9 | 10 |

When you think about how the world and your life will change over the next ten years, are you <u>mostly worried</u> or <u>mostly optimistic</u>?

Rate your outlook on a scale from 1 to 10.
1 is extremely worried, 10 is extremely optimistic.

| 1 | 2 | 3 | 4 | 5 | 6 | 7 | 8 | 9 | 10 |

<u>How much control or influence</u> do you feel <u>you</u> personally have in determining how the world and your life changes over the next ten years?

Rate your outlook on a scale from 1 to 10.
1 is almost no control or influence. 10 is almost complete control or influence.

| 1 | 2 | 3 | 4 | 5 | 6 | 7 | 8 | 9 | 10 |

This can also be done using The Polak Game, created by sociologist Fred Polak,[29] which invites participants to position themselves on the floor, creating a 2x2 matrix in the room. On one axis you have the level of optimism/pessimism; on the other axis you have the level of agency (I can/cannot make a difference).

EXAMPLES OF USAGE

Pingala. This Danish IT consultancy has used The Polak Game as part of their scenario planning and Futurecasting exercises. (See detailed case description elsewhere in this book.) Asking people to line up according to their personal reflection on each Futures Outlook question creates a shared understanding of the group's overall outlook on the future. Polling the participants on these three questions, and asking them to position themselves in the room, is a fast and engaging method for collecting and discussing the perspectives. It only takes six minutes to get this shared insight.

Steno, The Steno Diabetes Centre Copenhagen. This Danish healthcare organization works to offer world-class treatment and promote better quality of life and health equality for people with diabetes, their relatives and the Danish general population. It has used this methodology internally, in surveys and in workshops. It solicited opinions and perspectives from employees on their Future Outlook for Steno, and the world in general. This was part of the design of a critical transformation of the approach to patient care, which touched virtually every part of the health care centre.

The point, apart from establishing a mutual group understanding, is to discuss both individual and organizational agency: The ability of a person or a group to shape their future.

Mapping your Temporal Anchoring, using the Futures Triangle
Temporal Anchoring refers to a mental bias, where we rely on a specific reference point in time (the 'anchor') to make judgments, take decisions, or form opinions about actions or scenarios.

Sohail Inayatullah invented the Futures Triangle as a tool for exploring the role that the past, present and future play in imagining possible futures.[30]

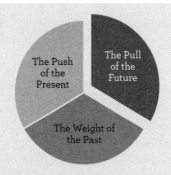

Figure 8
The Futures Triangle model by Sohail Inayatullah,
here represented as a pie chart

The Pull of the Future: Visions, trends, stories and other 'magnetic' ideas that pull you toward the future.

The Push of the Present: Trends, signals and forces (internally or externally) that push you, disturb you or motivate you right now.

The Weight of the Past: Habits, cultures, structures and other blockers that hinder you from moving toward a new future.

I am in the habit of using the pie chart layout, as pictured above, since it leaves more room for adding notes in a workshop setting.

First, **use the model with the three fields to capture** what is attractive about the future, what pushes you in the present and what weighs on you from the past.

Then, use the model to map and locate each **individual person's Temporal Anchoring** going into this transformation or change.

EXAMPLES OF USAGE

A healthcare organization used this tool in a workshop to let employees express their opinion on their current situation, the history they carried with them, and the possible change they were embarking on in one of their patient-focused departments. Some were clearly anchored in the past, remembering 'the good old days,' and some longed for a brighter, better future. This drove discussions about the underlying forces and drivers, helping them to enrich and improve both the change process and the co-created solution.

At **a life sciences organization**, in a workshop with participants from across the value chain focusing on reimagining possible scenarios for parts of the production process, they used the tool in the same way. This prompted discussion of what forces weigh down, pull or push, when the participants were mentally anchored in time.

The key take-away is a personal and shared reflection on the friction and gravity we experience when we're exposed to the idea of change and transformation.

WORKING WITH MULTIPLE FUTURES:
THE FUTURES CONE

The central concept in Futures Thinking is the plural 's' in futures. We work deliberately with multiple futures. Having a method for illustrating their characteristics and qualities supports us in our discussion of them.

This is where the Futures Cone, Futurecasting, Backcasting and Forecasting come into play.

In 1990, Charles Taylor, a strategic futurist from the Strategic Studies Institute at the US Army War College, described what he called 'The Cone of Plausibility.'[31] Physicist and strategic consultant Joseph Voros developed the so-called Futures Cone as a visual representation of the likelihood of different possible futures, represented as nested cones.[32]

These futures are described poetically, with alliteration, in ascending order, based on an increasing likelihood of happening:

- Potential: Everything beyond the present moment
- Preposterous: "Impossible! Won't ever happen!"
- Possible: Based on future knowledge. "Might happen"
- Plausible: Based on current knowledge. "Could happen"
- Probable: Based on current trends. "Likely to happen"
- Projected: The 'default' extrapolated 'baseline.' The 'business-as-usual' future

Adding an extra intersecting cone, representing the preferrable futures, will give us a way to describe both probability and preferences of scenarios.

- Preferable: Based on value judgments. "Want to happen. Should happen"

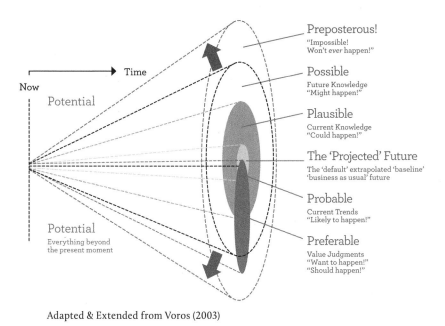

Adapted & Extended from Voros (2003)

Figure 9
The Futures Cone, as illustrated by Joseph Voros[33]

For practical applications, using possible, plausible and preferable futures for scenario building has shown to be good enough and useful for the majority of the transformations and change management planning endeavours. However, one can argue that impossible futures could be useful when discussing genuinely disruptive futures, as those futures or scenarios might become possible over time.

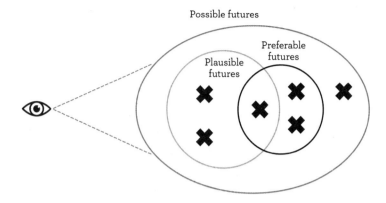

Figure 10
A simplified Futures Cone, focusing on possible,
plausible and preferable futures, based on the work
of Joseph Voros and his Futures Cone

Use this for creating a shared language, establishing the mental model of multiple futures and plotting out multiple scenarios within these futures. This can help acknowledge that plausible and preferable futures might not intersect in all cases, and guide discussion around what characteristics each of the areas have.

EXAMPLES OF USAGE

The Futures Cone was used at a Danish engineering company and by the **Novo Nordisk Facilitation** team, which supports the pharmaceutical multinational's leaders and employees in living up to their guiding principles, the so-called Novo Nordisk Way.

In both cases, the Futures Cone enabled them to: (a) Create a shared language of alternative futures; (b) Discuss the probability and desirability of such futures; (c) Address personal agency, the ability to act.

The Futures Cone and the embrace of multiple, alternative futures has also been a recurring element in the Good Morning April consultancy's 24-hour open hackathon each October, the **Hacktober**. We've used the tool to help people imagine possible (and impossible) futures, illustrate that change requires a deliberate adjustment in direction, and discuss the qualities and qualifiers of such alternative futures. For instance, what is the possibility of and preference for those futures, and what will alter your stance on that?

WORKING WITH THE MAGIC DUST:
TRENDS AND SIGNALS
In broad terms, working with the practical and cognitive process of Futures Thinking is a straightforward application of tools and techniques. The two crucial elements that make this distinctive are: (a) Yourself, and your organizational context; (b) The bulk of trends and signals that might affect you. Initiating the work with these trends and signals are to me an inflection point and a welcomed disruption in the work. This is also where we tackle head-on the emotions

related to the VUCAness and BANIness in and around you, as we establish a framework for discussing our points of view in a structured way.

I cannot stress enough the importance of this step.

Definition of megatrends, trends, signals and their variants
Let's get the definitions in place.

Term	Short description
Megatrend	A large, transformative trend with global impact and long duration, stable even in turbulent times. These are typically almost irreversible.
Trend	A general direction of change over time, identifiable in societal, technological, economic, environmental and political (STEEP) domains.
Signal	Concrete, observable evidence in the present that hints at future trends, such as anormal events, new technologies or surprising policies.
Driver	Underlying forces that shape future trends, including broad, long-term phenomena like climate change or demographic shifts.
Wild Card	Low-probability, high-impact events that are unpredictable but can dramatically change the future landscape.
Black Swan	Rare, high-impact events that are unexpected and hard to predict, with explanations that make them seem predictable in hindsight.

Figure 11
The definitions of megatrends, trends,
signals and their variants

Copenhagen Institute for Futures Studies describes Megatrends and Trends as follows:[34]

Megatrends: Long-term trajectories that for the most part stay their course, even in turbulent times. We can use megatrends to see the long-term picture through the short-term fog of uncertainty and rapid change. A rule of thumb is that a megatrend must be global in scope and unfold with relative certainty over a long period of time. Examples include globalization and economic growth, which have both been relatively stable in recent history.

Trends: Directions of change over time that are either increasing or decreasing in strength or frequency. Futurists typically study patterns of change in the STEEP categories to determine normal trends or baselines. These are then probed and examined, often using scenarios to challenge them and imagine alternative outcomes. Countertrends often emerge in response or opposition to the dominant trend.

Institute for the Future describes signals and drivers in the following way:[35]

Signals are evidence of the future that we can find in today's world. They are concrete, compelling observations about how the world is changing that give us a hint at where we might be headed. Think specific products, policies, events or experiences. The compelling element of signals should not be taken lightly. True signals incite a notable reaction, prompting us to pause and think about the possibilities they represent. Strong signals are essential for generating strong forecasts, as they allow futurists to provide grounded detail about new and unexpected experiences, behaviours and values.

Drivers, on the other hand, are broad, long-term trends that are likely to have a significant impact on the future. Examples of prominent drivers in today's world are climate change, the ageing population, proliferating disinformation and decreasing trust in government. Drivers provide critical context for analysing signals, as they allow practitioners to understand both the context through which a signal came to be and the implications a signal might have for the future.

Variants of these categorizations appear frequently in the professional literature and among futurists, including **Wild Cards** and **Black Swans** — the latter term coined by mathematician and risk analyst Nassim Nicholas Taleb[36] — which describe low-probability/high-impact events.

Having this broader list of definitions makes it possible for us to filter and focus on the elements that have a manageable level of impact and inertia on us. They are elements we have a reasonable opportunity to take into account when we engage in Futures Thinking and change management.

> **The terms with the highest degree of usefulness to us are trends and signals,** as they affect us at a level of magnitude where we can act, react, counteract or non-act in response to the impact this development might have.
>
> Trends and signals are within our 'circle of influence' — our ecosystem.

Two questions then arise:

First, where do I get a list of the trends and signals that are relevant to me?

Second, how do I use them?

Crafting your list of trends and signals

When engaging in Futures Thinking and working with multiple futures, the Magic Dust you put into your process and tools is the list of trends and signals that might have an impact on you and your organization. To come up with that list, you need a few guiding principles:

First, look at multiple domains simultaneously. You'll rarely be able to isolate your investigation and exploration to a single domain, like healthcare, as multiple descriptors are at play at the same time.

Let's say you work at a hospital and want to explore how patient care could be designed in the future. Here, you need to look at the future of healthcare, of technology, of health economics, and maybe more.

Second, get input from multiple sources. For instance, here are the sources I generally use:

- **Periodicals (hardcopy and digital)** from legitimate, reputable publishers and institutions. Many credible sources provide free and subscription-based access to valuable content. All the large consulting firms release thoroughly-researched, well-written reports on trends and signals. The World Economic Forum, UNESCO and OECD publish similar material, as do many futurists and change management practitioners, universities and national governments.

- **The news media, newsletters, online forums and similar outlets.** Paying attention to the news is a cheap resource for spotting trends and patterns and seeing signals. Subscribing to newsletters from futurists is an easy way to get fresh input, as is lurking and participating in online forums like */r/Futurology* on Reddit. Here, a healthy degree of both curiosity and scepticism is useful, to filter out scams, fake reporting or passionate screeds written in the heat of the moment.

- **Ask people**, ranging from family and friends to colleagues in your organization. Listen to what they see, experience and react to. Anecdotes can be a wonderful source for signals, and can reveal underlying movements and changes that might be useful, or destructive, to your transformation and change management. Rupert Hofmann from Audi Business Innovation calls these people **Trend Receivers**,[37] and has designed a robust concept for managing and nurturing this source of information.
- **Ask the Large Language Models (LLMs)**, such as ChatGPT, Copilot or Perplexity, for input. Use a prompt like, 'I'm looking for top-10 trends and signals regarding the future of sustainability, especially when it comes to the life sciences domain. Give me the answer in table format, include a short description, and include a signal strength for each of them. Also, describe the stakeholder groups that are impacted by this. Finally, add the internal functions in a life sciences organization that should be engaged in this.' It has been widely reported that LLMs can 'hallucinate' — technical glitches can generate false or misleading information, called confabulations — but in my experience the results are very useful as conversation starters.

A variant of these trends and signals are the internal signals, those that appear and emerge inside your organization. We will pay special attention to these, as they might have a direct impact on the scenarios, on the Anticipatory Assumptions, on the myths, and thus on the transformation and change management effort. We will dive into those later, especially regarding what to look for.

Along the way, **establish a rhythm and ritual of updating your list**. Your first attempt at compiling this list should not be your last. Make a habit of constantly sensing and scanning for trends and signals, looking for patterns and anomalies, and updating your list.

The methodology, called Horizon Scanning, is an integrated element in Futures Thinking. It describes in a metaphorical way of gazing into the horizon to get the first glimpses of the things that move toward us, or that we move toward. See *Safeguarding the Bioeconomy* by the National Academies of Sciences, Engineering and Medicine for a great overview of this structured approach.[38] Your results naturally improve with practice, better equipment and colleagues who can share their point of view.

Signal Sorting

With the list of relevant trends and signals at hand, the next step is to engage in an impact analysis. That is, discuss the impact that these trends and signals might have on your organization, and whether you like the effect they will have. Not all these trends will be relevant to your organization, in your context, with your people, and in your situation. And, you need to consider the bias and credibility of the source of the trend and signal. A trend identified in the US might not be relevant in Europe, and vice versa. At the same time, you might have different opinions based on where in your organization you are located, your life situation, your level of organizational consciousness, and your personal willingness to take risks. Remember the discussion on Future Outlook and Temporal Anchoring? This plays a role here.

A classic example of such an analysis tool is a 2x2 matrix, with two axes that guide your conversation. OECD plots low/high degree of influence and low/high degree of uncertainty on the axes.[39] Along with other variants, Copenhagen Institute for Futures Studies uses degree of uncertainty and degree of impact, and in 'Strategic Foresight' they suggest uncertainty and relevance.[40]

Personally, I have had success with a version of this, inviting participants to sort the trends and signals according to likelihood and likeability (the 'Double L'). I invite them to share their points of view on the probability and desirability of the effect of the trends and signals, aligned with UNESCO futurist Riel Miller's academic thoughts.[41]

The Double L tool works as follows:

THE DOUBLE L TOOL FOR SIGNAL SORTING

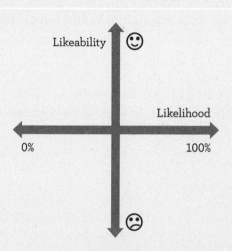

Figure 12
The Signal Sorting tool, focusing on
Likelihood and Likeability

Compile the list of trends and signals you want to explore.

For each of them, ask:

What is the **likelihood** of this trend/signal affecting us, in our context?

What is the **likeability** of the effect it would have on us, in our context?

Share your points of view, anecdotes and underlying assumptions.

Participants in this workshop overwhelmingly praise the learning they get from insights into each other's perspectives on the likelihood and likeability of these trends and signals. Additionally, this helps surface Anticipatory Assumptions, organizational myths and personal beliefs. This is the 'Double A' aspect, which we'll cover later in the book.

The Double L tool has significant effects on:
(a) Our transformation and change management design;
(b) Your leadership.

Ad (a): The concrete results from using the tool, the dialogue and mutual exchange of personal points of view, and the list of Anticipatory Assumptions, are vital elements in understanding and designing the transformation and the change management effort.

Ad (b): The Double L serves as a vehicle for nurturing and training your Anticipatory Leadership, especially as it sharpens your imagination, storytelling and ability to vocalize your underlying Anticipatory Assumptions.

EXAMPLES OF USAGE

This exercise is one of my personal favourites, for several reasons. It's easy to get started with, and it facilitates a ton of key discussions. It nudges the participants to share numerous anecdotes from their organizations, and is a wonderful way for people to have nuanced dialogues about trends, which they tend to accept as truths. And, it is a low-barrier gateway into further curiosity and engagement with the Using the Future approach.

Here are a few examples of situations where I've used Signal Sorting:

- At **Copenhagen Business School**, with a class of experienced business leaders studying for a Masters of Business Development degree
- With **Chiesi Farmaceutici**, an Italian pharmaceutical multinational, discussing the effect of sustainability trends in the pharma sector
- At **Novo Nordisk**, facilitating a dialogue on the Future of Work and its potential effect on cultural strategy
- With the global HR team in **a Danish manufacturer**, discussing how the trends within Future of Work affects HR professionals differently around the globe
- With 25 chief doctors and chief nurses from **multiple hospitals in Denmark**, discussing the impact of Future of Work trends on the culture and governance in a hospital setting
- At Good Morning April's 24-hour **Hacktober** workshop, enabling participants across numerous domains to share their perspectives on the trends and signals from technology and society that affect them

It can be revealing to create a heatmap across workshops that discuss the same trends and signals, to see how specific signals are distributed across the LIKELIHOOD and LIKEABILITY continuum.

Here is a heatmap across approximately 20 workshops, discussing these four signals:

- The employee (not the employer) takes control of Hybrid work
- The Metaverse is coming to our workplaces
- Cobots (collaborative robots) are entering our collaboration space with AI
- Extreme localization of cultures in organizations, as a replacement of global One Company cultures

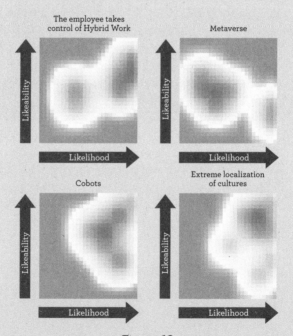

Figure 13
A heatmap, illustrating the distribution of Likelihood and Likeability over several applications of the tool

The distribution in the 2x2 matrix reveals strong differences in perspectives, which is a valuable input to the creation of plausible and preferable futures later in the Using the Future process.

Futures Wheel

Understanding the effects of a single trend or scenario is just as valuable as comparing them, as it unveils possible consequences, ripple effects, barriers and synergies in the trend/signal/ecosystem interplay.

My favourite tool to use in an organizational setting is the Futures Wheel, developed by social scientist and futurist Jerome C. Glenn in 1972.[42] The process entails a few steps, as illustrated below.

THE FUTURES WHEEL BY JEROME C. GLENN

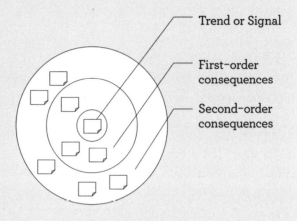

Trend or Signal

First-order
consequences

Second-order
consequences

Figure 14
The Futures Wheel tool

Identify the trend, signal, event, anomaly, Black Swan
or other phenomenon you want to investigate. Place it
in the middle of the Futures Wheel.

Now, let it unfold. Identify consequences of this trend/
signal. 'If *this* happens, then *that* happens as a result.'

Unfold the second-order consequences too ... and third-
order consequences.

You might want to colour-code the order or the
effects with similarities — for example, according to
technology, organization, collaboration or community.

Analyse the impact and what it means to you, your
organization and your transformation/change. It might
affect your solution or your way toward achieving it.

Again, listen for the Anticipatory Assumptions that emerge in the discussions, and add them to your list of organizational myths and beliefs.

EXAMPLES OF USAGE

At **Chiesi Farmaceutici**, the Futures Wheel was used to discuss and share perspectives on possible consequences of signals within sustainability in the pharma industry.

At **Hacktober**, participants shared their thoughts on the consequences of the broader trends in technology and society. As the groups were from mixed industry backgrounds (IT, pharma, banking, etc.) and from different functions in the organizations (HR, R&D, C-level), the cross-pollination helped them see things from different perspectives.

At **Steno Diabetes Centre Copenhagen**, the Futures Wheel was used as a tool to investigate ripple effects of transformative changes in their approach to patient care. (See the case study described elsewhere in this book.)

WORKING WITH SCENARIOS

A central element of Futures Thinking is establishing scenarios for alternative futures. These storylines support us in exploring and evaluating possible, plausible and preferable futures, by triggering emotional responses to them.

Scenarios are fictitious, and as such they spark our imagination and storytelling, strengthening our Anticipatory Leadership.

Futurecasting

The approach to building scenarios can be called Futurecasting. Futurecasting is different from traditional Forecasting and Backcasting in that it focuses on envisioning and shaping future scenarios rather than predicting or planning for specific outcomes. This is also called 'Standing in the Future.'

Futurecasting, as a form of scenario building, is the process of describing in detail how a future scenario might look. There's a consensus among futurists that the more detail you establish in a scenario, the more useful it is as a mechanism for us to explore it. Imagine describing the room you are in, who you are with, how you collaborate, what's on your desk, what you see out of your window, how it smells, what clothes you wear, how you commute, how you communicate, and so on.

Futurist and game designer Stuart Candy created a framework, The Experiential Futures Ladder,[43] to help structure one's scenario description from most abstract to most concrete:

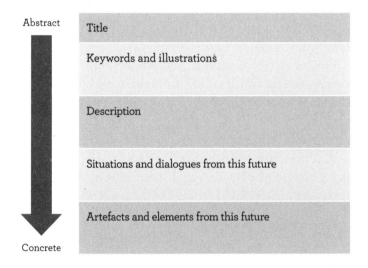

Figure 15
An adaptation of The Experiential Futures Ladder,
by Stuart Candy

Candy uses the term 'Experiential Threshold' to refer to the point where the description of the scenario becomes tangible and detailed. Such examples are **'artefacts from the future'** — things that might exist in that specific future. "Pick a room in the house and think what might exist in that room" and "pick an everyday activity and think how that might be different," as Institute for the Future prompts us in their training material.

There are various ways to structure or categorize the establishment of those scenarios. Here are a few relevant ones:

Thinking through **utopian/dystopian futures** is the classic Futurecasting approach. Describe a future where everything is great, positive, ideal, perfect. Similarly, describe a future where everything is miserable, negative, dysfunctional and broken. This is a standard way to discuss how projects can go right ... or go wrong.

Social scientist and futurist James Dator[44] categorized those projected futures into **four main images**: Continuation, Collapse, Disciplined Society and Societal Transformation.

Institute for the Future calls their version of four **alternative futures** Growth, Constraint, Collapse and Transformation.

Copenhagen Institute for Futures Studies cleverly uses the **Scenario Matrix**, devised in the 1990s by the consulting firm Global Business Network. The academic Alun Rhydderch[45] described the approach as follows: "This method generates up to four contrasted scenarios relevant to a particular area of interest (geographic or thematic) by placing two factors that influence the future of the issue under study on two axes which cross to form four quadrants." The key elements here are the trends, signals or drivers that we are investigating, each with polarities regarding their development over time (slow/fast, local/global, free/regulated, weak/strong, less/more, etc.).

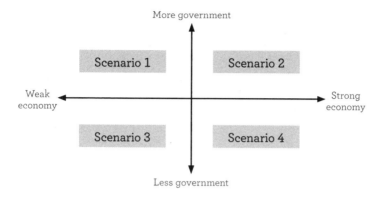

Factor 1: Strength of economy   Factor 2: Governance

Figure 16
An example of a 2x2 scenario matrix. Source: Alun Rhydderch,
'Scenario Building: The 2x2 Matrix Technique'

Regardless of how you approach scenario building and Futurecasting, the scenario must have a concise, catchy name and engaging description.

> Good, useful scenarios have a story and are memorable. Scenarios must be able to be communicated and visualized in a form that enables *other people* to engage with them, understand them, and have an emotional response to them.[46]

Again, this is a training ground for imagination and storytelling, both of which are crucial elements in the characteristics of Anticipatory Leadership.

And, make sure to update your list of myths, beliefs and Anticipatory Assumptions, as these will inevitably surface and emerge during the Futurecasting process.

Evaluating scenarios

The question then becomes how we pull together our emotional responses to the scenario. Evaluation of scenarios logically feeds into their placement in the Futures Cone.

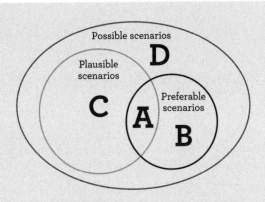

Figure 17
Scenarios with different characteristics,
according to plausibility and preference

How plausible is this scenario?

How preferable is this scenario?

Where should it be placed in the Futures Cone?

What will it take to move the scenario to another place on the map?

Note how the output from the Signal Sorting informs the scenarios, as the Likelihood/Likeability categorization has a resemblance to the Plausible/Preferable scenarios.

Other questions and discussions could be:
- How expensive is it to establish this scenario?
- How difficult?
- What does it require?
- Who might this be good for, if not for us?
- Who would love this scenario? Who would hate it?

The researchers Rhisiart, Miller and Brooks highlight two insights to gain from a structured process for learning and cognition, related to foresight and Strategic Foresight processes:[47]

1. Shared learning about the topic at hand, combined with insight into the trends and signals in that domain.
2. Building the mastery of Using the Future, especially around the capacity of Futures Literacy.

From my experience there are at least three additional significant gains to be made from building and evaluating scenarios:

3. Mutual insight into Anticipatory Assumptions, myths, biases and beliefs, both individual and organizational.
4. Greater hope, lower anxiety, stronger ownership and higher confidence about the future.
5. Activating agency in the participants, across the organization and throughout the ecosystem.

We will return to points 4 and 5 later in this book, where we focus on the emotional value creation of Using the Future and Anticipatory Leadership.

EXAMPLES OF USAGE

In a business unit in **a Danish biotech company** several scenarios for embracing New Ways of Working were established. Some were inspired by Teal, some we inspired by Agile and Scrum, and some through combining several trending methodologies.

To investigate the desirability of the scenarios in the organization, a handful of experiments were designed and executed over a five-month period, using a slightly adjusted test card/learning card approach from entrepreneur Alexander Osterwalder and marketing consultant David Bland.[48]

The results were used to zoom in on the design of single components in the scenarios, to refine placement in the scenario map (preferable and plausible), and subsequently to act on it.

At **another life sciences organization**, this approach was used to evaluate the scenarios for transformative changes to their core process. In a workshop, a few scenarios were identified, and experiments were initiated to investigate critical or sensitive parts over the following several months. This led to nominating the preferred scenario for the first phase of the transformation.

Backcasting – and Forecasting

Building a roadmap to your preferred future or scenario is the logical next step in the Futures Thinking process. As a vehicle for transformation and change management, participatory planning of actions is key, since it establishes ownership, responsibility and engagement.

There are two popular ways of doing this in Futures Thinking: Forecasting and Backcasting.

Forecasting is the process of 'making probabilistic statements about the future based on past and present data. Common applications for Forecasting are weather forecasts and economic forecasts.'[49] Forecasting entails casting yourself forward, starting from where you are, to predict and plan future events and actions.

Backcasting is 'a planning method that starts with defining a desirable future and then working backwards,' toward today.[50] Backcasting is the process of standing in the future, and then figuring out what it takes to walk backwards to the present.

Here is a comparison of the three casting elements we've introduced:

Aspect	1: Futurecasting	2: Backcasting	3: Forecasting
Focus	Envisioning and describing possible, plausible and preferable future scenarios	Working backwards from a preferred future to create strategies for reaching it	Predicting and planning future events and actions based on data and models
Nature of scenarios	Imaginative and speculative scenarios	Preferred futures and scenarios	Based on historical data and current trends
Methodology	Creative imagination and scenario building	Identifying constraints and developing strategies, working backwards	Quantitative and qualitative analysis, extrapolation and prediction
Data	Less reliant on historical data, more on creativity and points of view	Starts with future vision and assesses current state	Data-driven and historical analysis
Adaptability	More adaptable to changes, surprises, shifts and shocks	Adaptable to evolving circumstances	Less adaptable to unexpected changes

Figure 18
Comparing Futurecasting, Backcasting and Forecasting

Backcasting starts with deciding on a preferred future, followed by shared establishment of a mental reversed timeline, from the future back to the present. What follows is a series of brainstorms, discussions and identification of key elements that will help make that future come true.

BACKCASTING

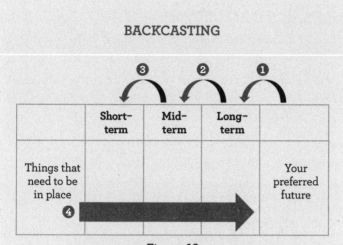

Figure 19
The Backcasting model, inspired by
Institute for the Future

Imagine your preferred future. Use the detailed description from the scenarios to immerse yourself in the setting, letting the emotional response set in.

Go backwards from the future.
What needs to happen right before that future?

Keep going backwards, to identify actions, capabilities, metrics and resources that need to be in place in each step.

When you end in the present, establish your actions, milestone plan and roadmap for your transformation and change.

As always, pay attention to imagination and storytelling, and the list of Anticipatory Assumptions that emerge during the process.

EXAMPLES OF USAGE

At **a Danish affiliate of a global life sciences organization,** Backcasting was used to identify critical elements in a five-year roadmap toward an envisioned future state.

The four-hour workshop was kicked off with a 'Standing in the Future' exercise, followed by group work to backcast from there, in waves of two years.

Backcasting was also used at **Roche**, **Pingala** and **Steno** to 'plan from the future, not from the present.' (See the case studies described elsewhere in this book.)

OTHER TOOLS
Although the tools I've listed have proven valuable in the organizational setting, and fit together and establish a smooth, coherent process with synergetic interfaces and logic, numerous other such tools exist.

Economist and futurist Rafael Popper created this 'Foresight Diamond':[51]

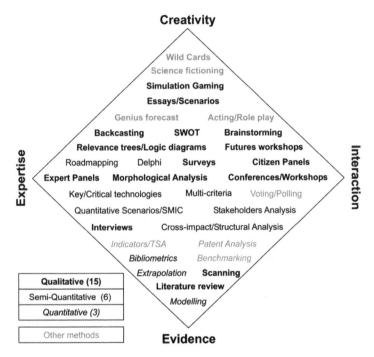

Source: Adapted from Popper (2008)

Figure 20
An overview of other Futures Thinking tools,
captured in the Foresight Diamond

Copenhagen Institute for Futures Studies suggests using their Copenhagen Method,™ which builds on several additional tools, like Driver Mapping, Trends Radar, Wind Tunneling and more.

Institute for the Future similarly adds simulation tools, leveraging the game designer Jane McGonigal's work: Alternative Futures simulations, Future Feelings map, Equitable Futures card game, Artefacts from the Future, and more.

A long list of tools is also available in *Strategic Foresight*,[52] including the Delphi Method.

> Wonderfully and overwhelmingly, many tools and methodologies exist, all to help you in Using the Future to make better decisions today.
>
> Mostly, it's a matter of familiarizing yourself with the tools that spark your interest and support you, your transformation and your leadership.

TRENDS AND SIGNALS, SENSED AND RECEIVED
BY JEFF JENSEN
Founder, Xronos Inc.

Location: USA

- Clear tendency toward momentum. "The regular cadence of work increases." Wait-time decreases, as companies focus on outcome.

- Risk-taking decreases. Investment in innovation decreases. Typical timeframe for innovation cycles gets shorter.

- Fear of AI. Attempts to ban ChatGPT at work for coding. "... but life will find a way," he says with a wink.

WHAT IS FUTURES LITERACY?

Futures Literacy is the ability and capacity to think critically and abstractly about the future. Key building blocks are the understanding of anticipation and assumptions.

Futures Thinking is the creative and investigative process of exploring and evaluating what affects us, to describe scenarios for the futures.

As previously mentioned, Futures Literacy and Futures Thinking are closely related concepts, as the mindset and mechanisms support each other, both in terms of philosophy and discovery. Working diligently with the tools strengthens your ability and capacity to be a futures literate person, or organization, juggling and navigating the Futures Thinking methodology with agility and coherence. The learning in one area seeps into the other.

FUTURES LITERACY IS BOTH HOW AND WHY
According to UNESCO's Riel Miller, "A futures literate person has acquired the skills needed to decide why and how to use their imagination to introduce the non-existent futures into the present."[53]

Miller, along with researchers Nicklas Larsen and Jeanette Kæseler Mortensen, describes in a paper how Futures Literacy is "the capacity to know how to imagine the future, and why it is necessary."[54]

They underline that Futures Literacy is not only about mastering abstract, critical thinking, but also knowing the approaches, tools and mechanisms. They note that it's also about WHY you would want to imagine the futures and use them actively and diligently, and WHY using your imagination works. This is a powerful point, which I think is lost in several of the sources in the field.

> Being Futures Literate is also knowing **WHY** you would want to use the future.
>
> It is mastering HOW to, WHY it works and WHY you should engage in it.

Being aware of your society and community, paying attention to trends and emerging movements, and sensing the unspoken and unwritten are all means to imagining where and how the world could and should be better. The scope can be in your home, local community, country, the planet, the universe, and within your organization, business unit or team. At work, it helps you sense emerging developments, and enables you to form an opinion on what changes are needed, and what the future state could look like, while supporting you in transformation and change management.

To some of the people I've met in Futures Literacy courses and seminars, this is a human, philosophical and spiritual responsibility: To plan for a future we want to be part of.

FRAMEWORK AND BUILDING BLOCKS OF FUTURES LITERACY

Futures Literacy does not provide solutions. It provides insight, uncovers beliefs and biases, and establishes a shared understanding and language. It prepares you for thinking critically and abstractly, allowing you to reveal, reframe and rethink your Anticipatory Assumptions.

Anticipation and assumptions are fundamental building blocks in Futures Literacy.

"The future does not exist in the present but anticipation does.
The form the future takes in the present is anticipation."
— Riel Miller[55]

Merriam-Webster defines anticipation as "the act of looking forward" and "visualization of a future event or state." Assumption is "a fact or statement (...) taken for granted." These are closely related to biases and beliefs. Here is a brief overview of the different components, and their role in Futures Thinking and Futures Literacy:

	Description	Role in Futures Thinking and Futures Literacy
Anticipations	Expectations or predictions about future events, scenarios or outcomes.	Can help in envisioning possible future scenarios and evaluating trends and signals. Can shape the foundation upon which possible, plausible and preferable futures are built.
Assumptions	Things taken for granted or accepted as true without explicit evidence or confirmation.	
Biases	Systematic and often unconscious tendencies to favour or disfavour certain ideas, groups or outcomes.	Can lead to distorted views of the future if not addressed and accounted for. Can influence one's perspective on what is desirable or possible in the future.
Beliefs	Personal convictions that ideas are true or real, often rooted in faith, knowledge or personal experience.	
Myths	Widely shared but possibly false beliefs that influence the behaviour and decision-making processes within organizations.	

Figure 21
Descriptions of anticipations, assumptions, biases, beliefs and myths

In Futures Literacy, two different forms of anticipation are used to describe and categorize the thinking: Anticipation for the Future vs. Anticipation for Emergence.

Anticipation for the Future is the traditional way of contemplating what's to come, often based on forecasts, trends and desired images of the future. On the other hand, Anticipation for Emergence is about welcoming uncertainty and changes, focusing on adaptation and playing it by ear, and on sensing, sense-making and uncovering novelty.

UNESCO's Miller has thoroughly described the framework in his book, *Transforming the Future – Anticipation in the 21st Century*, from which I cite the following:

On Anticipation for the Future:

"The 'being' of Anticipation-for-the-Future is the future as a goal — a planned/desired future that people bet on."

"Anticipation-for-the-Future is the frame that legitimises and incentivises the grandiose claims being made by leaders worldwide that they can impose their will on tomorrow. In a nutshell, the imperative is to colonise tomorrow with today's idea of tomorrow."

On Anticipation for Emergence:

"The future of Anticipation-for-Emergence is one that is not a goal or target meant to structure the making of preparatory and planning Anticipation-for-Emergence. The later-than-now imagined in Anticipation-for-Emergence is a disposable construct, a throwaway non-goal that need not be constrained by probability or desirability."

"Anticipation-for-Emergence is a use of the future to sense and make sense of aspects of the present, particularly novelty, which tends to be obscured by Anticipation-for-the-Future."

We can tie this back to the previous discussion about Settling into the future or Exploring the future:

> Anticipation for the Future is what a Settler applies.
> Anticipation for Emergence is what an Explorer applies.

Miller stresses how the two forms of anticipation support each other, highlighting the so-called primary hypothesis in the research field:

"When people engage in a knowledge creation process designed to imagine the future in the form of Anticipation-for-Emergence it is easier to: (1) sense and make-sense of existing but otherwise invisible emergent-novelty, and (2) invent or innovate — the actual creation of emergent-novelty. The proposition is that imagining Anticipation-for-Emergence futures makes it easier for people to: invent new words; sense and make-sense of the novel; imagine the potential for the persistence of changes that are always initially locally unique and seemingly ephemeral; and pose questions that are new because they can detect and invent phenomena that make up the emergent present, including new paradigms."

He captures the framework in the illustration below, categorizing the different applications and approaches to Using the Future, and how Anticipatory Assumptions (AA) appear.

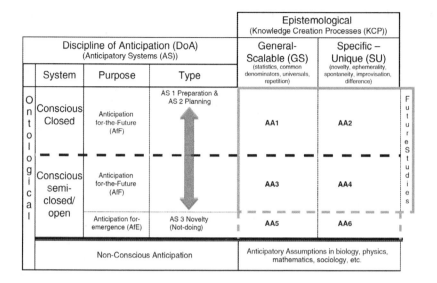

Figure 22
A framework for describing and researching
Futures Literacy, by Riel Miller in Transforming
the Future: Anticipation in the 21st Century

Futures Literacy helps us formulate how we use the future, and why. The key points in Futures Literacy can be summarized as:

- The future only exists as imagination and storytelling
- Using the Future is about producing fiction
- By exploring those fictitious futures, we uncover our (Anticipatory) Assumptions
- Futures Literacy is also about sensing what emerges
- Your imagination process can have different starting points and directions, affected by what intent you have — Settling or Exploring

TOOLS AND MECHANISMS OF FUTURES LITERACY

The following is a small collection of the tools and mechanisms that are useful in a business setting, when applying Futures Literacy to your transformation and in your change management.

The overall process and approach are described at the end of this chapter, assembling it all into an approach I've mentioned a few times earlier, called 'Double L Double A Double E.'

This chapter is influenced by books and training I've participated in, especially the courses at Copenhagen Institute for Futures Studies, The Emergence Academy at Hawkwood Centre for Future Thinking, and the Futures Literacy Labs I have codesigned and taken part in. (See Recommended Reading, Listening and Watching, later in the book, for further details.)

THE FUTURES LITERACY LAB

A Futures Literacy Lab is a practical, well-defined framework for revealing, reframing and rethinking the Anticipatory Assumptions that are used to imagine the futures. It was developed by UNESCO as an action-learning tool, to shape coursework and provide input to scientific studies on Futures Thinking and Futures Literacy.

I will only give an overview here, as both the UNESCO website and the academic and consultant Jan Oliver Schwarz, in *Strategic Foresight*, have described it in detail.

The Futures Literacy Lab has three-plus-one phases that are diligently and carefully designed to the situation, context, participants and timeframe. A lab can last from an hour to a two-day immersive experience. All labs require: (a) A selected future that you want to explore; (b) A chosen timeframe;

(c) A carefully crafted 'reframe' — a new future to work with — to be used in Phase 2.

Examples of the future to investigate can be broad:
- The future of healthcare in ten years
- The future of identity in 50 years
- The future of pandemics in 70 years

Or, very specific:
- The future of banking in Denmark in 20 years, if the proposal for abandoning cash becomes a reality
- The future of agriculture in 20 years, if development of electric vehicles continues, leading to a massive drop in demand for crops used for production of ethanol, which is mixed into gasoline[56]

From there, the lab unfolds with workshop approaches and components that should be designed to suit the situation, as depicted below.

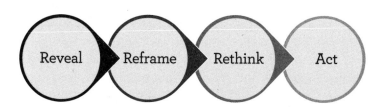

Figure 23
The four phases of a Futures Literacy Lab

Phase 1: Reveal
- Goal: To reveal your assumptions
- What is the probable future? What do you think is going to happen?
- What is the preferable future? What do you hope is going to happen?
- As you work, note down your assumptions and myths

Phase 2: Reframe
- Goal: To reframe your assumptions
- Participants will be given a reframe intended to challenge assumptions, making them 'imagine the future of the topic through a frame that is unfamiliar and distinct from the ones revealed in Phase 1'[57]
- Given this alternative future, what is my first response? What am I being challenged on? What assumptions are challenged? What changes?
- This is meant to challenge our assumptions, change the assumptions, and create new and reframed assumptions
- Note: This reframe is crucial, and requires some attention to genuinely challenge assumptions of the probable future

Phase 3: Rethink
- Goal: To rethink your assumptions
- Back in the present, what new questions arise regarding the probable and preferable futures?
- How has your perception changed? What do you see differently? What new issues have emerged during the process? How many 'what if ...' questions can you create?

Phase 4: Act
- Goal: To turn the learning into action
- What actions does that create?
- What do you need to explore?

As inspiration, a long list of Futures Literacy Labs can be found on UNESCOs website, including YouTube videos.

From my experience with these workshops, there are four helpful activities that can be baked into running such labs in your organization:

1. Shared training and learning on the theory and practice of Futures Literacy.
2. Training and learning on Futures Literacy as an individual and organizational capacity.
3. Spelling out specific actions to take and engage in.
4. The unveiling of Anticipatory Assumptions, biases, beliefs and myths.

APPROACHES TO UNCOVER AND DISCUSS ANTICIPATORY ASSUMPTIONS

The second part of the 'Double L Double A Double E' approach focuses on uncovering and discussing Anticipatory Assumptions, and their related aspects: biases, beliefs and myths.

Economist and futurist Stefan Bergheim conducted a study across 11 Futures Literacy Labs, to document the 500 Anticipatory Assumptions that arose and investigate patterns via an inductive qualitative content analysis. The result was published in a paper, *Patterns of Anticipatory Assumptions.*[58]

He categorized the assumptions in 18 categories, as illustrated below.

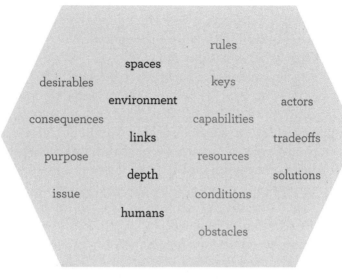

Basics **Dimensions** *Dis-/Enablers* *Change*

Source: Stefan Bergheim

Figure 24
The Futures Assumptions Hexagon, by Stefan Bergheim

Bergheim describes the categories as follows:
- **basic categories** with assumptions about
  › The **issue** of the [workshop], the **purpose** of the [workshop], the **consequences** of (not) doing anything, and about **desirable** futures.
- Next are categories of assumptions about the different **dimensions** of the topic:
  › about **human** nature, about the **depth** of the issue, the **links** to neighbouring issues, the larger **environment** in which the topic is situated, and the **spaces** where things are happening on the topic.

- The third meta-category includes assumptions about **dis-/enablers** that prepare the ground for the later exploration of actions:
  - › The **obstacles** identified, the **conditions** for change, the **capabilities** and **resources** required, as well as assumptions about the **key** to change and the **rules** that are at play.
- Finally, the meta-dimension of **change** includes more concrete assumptions about
  - › **Solutions**, potential **tradeoffs**, and **actors**.

Examples of Anticipatory Assumptions, adapted from Bergheim:
- Trust is underrated in the leadership team
- Cooperation brings better results in terms of diversity
- People need other people to feel acknowledged
- Leadership is a constant struggle
- There is always a role for an educator on the team
- Time is a precious resource
- Technology is moving people apart
- Working together is essential for belonging
- There is enough budget to be able to implement the improvements
- Technology is THE enabler of organizational democracy
- All departments will be willing to adopt the same governance framework
- Learning is becoming more individualized
- We prefer autonomy over alignment
- The younger generation is leading the change

From that we can see that one way to verbalize and describe the Anticipatory Assumptions is to use the structure of a noun, a verb and a descriptor.

> Verbalize the Anticipatory Assumptions with a noun, a verb and a descriptor.
>
> Capture them in a log.

Apart from the Futures Literacy Lab, several well-known tools exist to uncover anticipation, assumptions, biases, beliefs and myths. Here is a list of ten tools that I find useful in a business setting, for learning Futures Literacy and applying to change management activities:

1. **Future Outlook/Temporal Anchoring/Futures Triangle survey:** A way to probe and discuss your futures-readiness.
2. **Scenario planning/Futurecasting:** A method to create, explore and evaluate different future scenarios to understand potential outcomes. (See previous chapter in this book.)
3. **Signal Sorting:** Discussing the likelihood/likeability of the impact of a signal, the 'Double L.'
4. **Delphi method:** Involves collecting expert opinions through anonymous iterative surveys or discussions to reach a consensus on future possibilities.
5. **Wild cards/Black Swan analysis:** Identifying and preparing for extreme, low-probability events that could have a significant impact on the future.
6. **Futures Wheel:** A visual tool for exploring consequences and implications of events. (See previous chapter.)
7. **Pre-mortem analysis:** Imagining a future failure scenario and examining the assumptions that might have led to it.

8. **Bias surveys:** Using surveys or questionnaires to uncover cognitive biases and preferences among participants.
9. **Advisory Boards:** Inviting internal or external experts or teams to critically assess and challenge internal assumptions, biases and myths.
10. **Cultural sensitivity training:** Raising awareness of cultural biases that may influence how individuals perceive and analyse future possibilities, which can be done using the Country Comparison Tool from Hofstede Insights as a starting point.

A strong piece of advice is to have one dedicated person in the workshop assigned to listen for and document statements that describe myths or Anticipatory Assumptions.

Examples of concrete entries in such a log, which I have experienced in real-life settings, are:

- 100% allocation to projects will never happen
- Management is reluctant to change
- Management changes too much, too often
- The strategy is carved in stone and cannot be influenced
- These megatrends will never affect us in our department
- The finance department is anchored in the past
- The global HR strategy is inefficiently 'one-size-fits-all'
- Employees will never embrace AI as a tool
- We're all going to be fired

DOUBLE A – ANTICIPATORY ASSUMPTIONS

Anticipatory Assumptions

Anticipatory assumptions form the foundation of our mental models, shaping our imagination, storytelling and anticipation of the future, and thus shape our actions in the present.

Often hidden, implicit or habitual, our underlying stories, values, beliefs, biases and myths are both personal and organizational in character.

Unveil them via workshops and dialogue.
Capture them in a log.
Discuss them.
Challenge them.
Disprove or verify them.

Use them throughout your transformation and change management, in your storytelling and engagement.

As described earlier, **Futures Literacy is the ability and capacity** to think critically and abstractly about the future.

HOW and WHY you do this is important.

How is about revealing, reframing and rethinking Anticipatory Assumptions.

Why is about understanding the insight the methodology establishes, and your personal call to action, in society and your organization.

REFLECTIONS FROM PART TWO

What are Futures Thinking and Futures Literacy, and what tools and mechanisms are useful for transformation and change management inside the organization?

Futures Literacy is the ability and capacity to think critically and abstractly about the future. Key building blocks are the understanding of anticipation and assumptions.

Futures Thinking is the creative and investigative process of exploring and evaluating what affects us, to describe scenarios for the futures.

Being futures literate is not only mastering the processes and tools, but also knowing WHY you would want to use the future. It is mastering HOW to, WHY it works, and WHY you should engage in it.

SUMMARY

The chapter introduces the terminology, definitions, mechanisms and tools that are applicable for the use of Futures Thinking inside the organization.

Using the Future: To explore and evaluate future scenarios, to make decisions today.

Strategic Foresight: Combines methods from futures studies with those used in strategic management. The chapter also raises the thought, 'Maybe we should start talking about **tactical foresight** instead.'

A variety of tools and **mechanisms for Futures Thinking** are presented: Futures-readiness, Futures Cone, Trends and signals, Futures Wheel, Scenarios, Futurecasting, Backcasting and Forecasting.

Similarly, **mechanisms for Futures Literacy** are introduced: The Futures Literacy Lab, and the approach to investigating Anticipatory Assumptions.

The chapter gives insight into the world of Futures Thinking and Futures Literacy, preparing you for PART THREE — applying it to your organization.

TRENDS AND SIGNALS, SENSED AND RECEIVED BY ELSE MARIE AGGER HANSEN

Vice President, Novo Nordisk
(These are Hansen's personal views,
and not an official view or statement of Novo Nordisk)

Location: Denmark, with an international presence

- After a period with aspirational direction setting/big themes, we seem to be moving toward very tangible, concrete goals; goals you can measure. Somewhat less focus on experimentation but more focus on delivering.

- Maybe as a consequence of the above, there is also less experimentation with the way we work. The interest in New Ways of Working has declined.

- Big focus on providing equal opportunities for people. This is a request coming from employees, and it goes very much beyond just gender equality. It can also be personality types (extraverts/introverts).

- More democratic educational programs. Previously, we had a range of talent programs employees would be appointed to by their Line of Business. Now, more courses are out in the open and free for everyone to participate in. I guess this goes hand-in-hand with more training being available through online programs. The new 'luxury' course is one where you actually participate in person.

- Due to the growth of our company, and in particular our global presence, there is a steep increase in organizational complexity which the employees have to navigate. This also dramatically impacts the way we work, with more online meetings, meetings spread out during the day, including in the evening, issues with when it is OK/not OK having meetings, problems with work-life balance, particularly for those with small kids, etc.

- AI is everywhere and everybody recognizes that this will revolutionize the way we work. Very few have a clue what it will change, just that this will dramatically change the way we work and that we all need to prepare and be more IT-skilled in general.

CASE STUDY: REIMAGINING THE FUTURE OF PATIENT CARE AT STENO, A DIABETES HEALTHCARE CENTRE

Who

Steno Diabetes Centre Copenhagen is a healthcare facility that offers treatment and contributes to quality of life and health equality for people with diabetes, their families and the Danish general population.

They take care of some 11,000 children and adults with diabetes from the Copenhagen area, of which 5,700 visit the centre annually.

The history of Steno goes back to 1932. The centre currently employs around 500 nurses, doctors, lab technologists, clinicians, psychologists, anthropologists, administrative personnel and others.

Elements from 'Using the Future'
- Futures Readiness
- Temporal Anchoring
- Standing in the Future
- Internal Signals
- Futures Wheel
- Scenarios and Futurecasting
- Explore and evaluate
- Backcasting and roadmap
- Anticipatory Assumptions and myths

Approach

How do you reimagine patient care, while taking trends in healthcare, society, leadership, work and technology into consideration?

This was the question the project group took up, when tasked by the leadership team and board of directors with rethinking and rebuilding patient care of the future. The 'Steno Life' program was initiated to establish an individualized, digitally assisted, needs-driven, modern outpatient centre for diabetes.

One department had already used elements from the Futures Thinking toolbox in redesigning parts of their organization, focusing on teaming, collaboration, distributed leadership and embracing change. During this transformation project, the Temporal Anchoring/Futures Triangle was used to map out what affected their personal stance toward change, and where they perceived themselves being anchored: in the past, the present or the future. Later, they used Standing in the Future exercises to imagine and tell stories about the future they wanted to be part of.

Having experienced firsthand the concrete results and emotional impacts of applying these few tools, the group adopted Using the Future in the larger-scale Steno Life transformation project.

The first workshops circled around understanding the transformation and establishing a shared picture of the business justification of the change.

Then, a series of Standing in the Future workshops were created, engaging the leadership team, responsible middle managers and internal collaboration partners to imagine the possible scenarios for patient care, three years from the present. The same workshop was held with patients, to get their input as well. Criticisms, scepticism, possibilism and hopefulness were aired during these meetings, as they sketched out plausible, and preferable, alternative futures, providing valuable insights into both subcomponents and full-picture scenarios.

A few weeks later, a daylong, business unit-wide Standing in the Future workshop was held, engaging 130 nurses, lab technicians, doctors, clinicians, biomedical laboratory scientists and other personnel with direct patient contact. They discussed the situation, created scenarios and illustrated them in drawings and with cardboard boxes or LEGO blocks. Throughout the day, a journalist and an anthropologist affiliated with the centre followed their work, capturing the experiences, emotional responses and group dynamics.

Special attention was given to listening for Anticipatory Assumptions, leading to the creation of a Myth Log with 45 outspoken myths. These were aggregated into a handful of distinct, often sceptical, opinions and perceptions of the transformation that the project group considered. They revealed the stories, reframed the assumptions and busted the myths, in line with the Futures Literacy Lab design.

Slowly but steadily, scenarios and subcomponents began emerging, with various traits. Some were plausible, but not appealing. Conversely, others were desirable, but not realistic.

Some had their focus on the clinicians and the in-house workstreams. Others had the new technology and wearables in focus. A bunch of them focused on cross-sector collaboration and society. Some zoomed in on self-lead teams and on decision-making processes related to the patient, to research, or to how to spend time. And yet others looked at the treatment regime, from the side of the patient considering the need for individualized profiling and planning for care and treatment.

One way the project group analysed, explored and evaluated these was to apply the Futures Wheel to subcomponents, to better understand the first-order and second-order consequences, and share opinions and perspectives on those futures that emerged. What was the likelihood of this becoming a reality? And what would be the likeability of the effects?

All this — the initial 'ask' for Steno Life, the business justification description, the multiple inputs to scenarios and alternative futures, and the myths — was taken into consideration when determining an approach and two preferred scenarios. In a two-day offsite session, the leadership team took part in exploring and evaluating these scenarios, pressure-testing them, identifying elements to initially establish, and ideas to experiment with. They backcasted from the future to plan for the first go-live, and laid out an iterative approach for following up with enhanced versions of Steno Life.

Now began the intense work of understanding the consequences for internal structures, cultures and governance in light of the scenarios, and the well-crafted activities for training, communication and change enablement, which would also include the patients.

Having mentally 'been to the future' enabled the team to imagine and discuss the best approaches to the execution, bringing Version 1 of Steno Life to life more vividly.

Outcome and impact

This approach is an example of 'strategizing and planning from the future,' not from the present. It entails Using the Future to make decisions for today, considering trends and movements in patient care, technology, leadership, work and society.

Apart from continuously monitoring the assumptions and myths, each workshop and meeting was closed with a 'confidence vote,' inviting all participants to share how convinced they were of the ultimate success of the project. The more involved people were, the more mandate they were asked to govern, and the more confidence was observed, indicating that ownership, agency and confidence are correlated emotional factors.

INTERLUDE: THE OBSERVATORY AND THE LABORATORY

This first appeared in 'Futures of Work: Horizon Scanning Document 2023,' published that year by Good Morning April, and has been adapted for the context here.[59]

In an observatory, you peer through a telescope at things that are very distant. You observe, take notes and try to understand. Maybe you spot something odd that makes you go 'huh.' Perhaps you see a pattern, or something new that either provides answers or prompts questions.

In the same way, Futures Thinking is a sort of observatory where we perceive behaviour and developments that are new to us. We scan the horizon to see those things that are approaching us. We take notes, wonder and try to understand.

In the observatory, we explore.

In a laboratory, on the other hand, you perform experiments to learn all kinds of things. For example, you examine context, causality and correlation. You formulate a hypothesis, analyse and synthesize your findings. This is where you conduct controlled experiments to understand primary effects, unwanted side effects, challenges in upscaling the experiment, and what risks there might be.

In the same way, Futures Thinking is a laboratory where you can experiment with the effects of trends and signals.

Structured approaches to imagination and real-life experimentation can help you understand possible futures and support you in spotting the preferred futures.

In the laboratory, we evaluate.

This analogy is greatly simplified, and does not fully recognize the complexity and value creation in those professional areas. But as a vehicle for understanding — and for communication with your peers and stakeholders — it's a nice way to set the scene for Futures Thinking in your organization.

PART THREE:

HOW TO APPLY FUTURES THINKING INSIDE YOUR ORGANIZATION

Next, I want to tackle the first three of the four questions that this book set out to answer:

- How do I use my understanding of trends and signals in society and technology to design my organization, culture and governance?
- How do I look for signals inside the organization?
- How do I challenge and revisit our assumptions and myths, upon which we build our view of the future?

The fourth question — what kind of anticipatory leadership it takes to be futures literate inside the organization — will be handled in the last part of the book.

Here, in PART THREE, we flip all these tools and mechanisms to the inside of the organization, to support us in transformations, change management and shaping our structures, cultures and governance.

> We want to use Futures Thinking on the inside
> of our organizations, applied to transformation
> and change management.

Special attention will be given to:

- How the approach changes when we flip it to the inside
- The overall method, 'Double L Double A Double E'
- Looking for internal signals
- Working with Anticipatory Assumptions and organizational myths
- The hypotheses-driven approach to exploring and evaluating the scenarios
- How the scenarios affect your structures, cultures and governance

WHAT CHANGES WHEN WE USE FUTURES THINKING INSIDE THE ORGANIZATION?

A few crucial topics are significantly different when we apply the methodology of Futures Thinking to the inside of our organization.

Topics	Using Futures Thinking for Strategic Foresight, on the <u>outside</u> of the organization	Using Futures Thinking for transformations, on the <u>inside</u> of the organization
Aim	To explore and evaluate how global (mega)trends affect the ecosystem of the organization, and the market, products and services they operate with	To explore and evaluate how external AND internal trends affect the business unit inside the organization, especially regarding how they work, their structures, their cultures and their governance
Business application	Strategic Management	Transformation and Change Management
Time horizon	Long-term — 10-20 years	Medium-term — 3-5 years
Scope	The market-facing parts of the organization — the 'outside,' where products and services meet customers, vendors, sub-contractors, regulatory bodies, the competition and the global infrastructure	Typical scope is your business unit, change initiative, organizational transformation, or something similar with: (a) Primarily internal interfaces; (b) Characteristics of a significant and intentional change in the structures, cultures, processes or master plan

Topics	Using Futures Thinking for Strategic Foresight, on the outside of the organization	Using Futures Thinking for transformations, on the inside of the organization
Origin of trends and signals	External	External and internal
Ownership	Top management, strategy team, marketing staff and innovation function	The business unit leadership team, change leads, transformation leads
Orientation	Toward the market	Toward the organization

Figure 25
Comparing the application of Futures Thinking for Strategic Foresight versus for transformation inside the organization

I know that these are rough and at times too-sharp distinctions, but they serve as guidelines for the design of the approach in these chapters, and as a mental model for the narrative.

USING THE FUTURE FOR CHANGE MANAGEMENT

'Using the Future' is the central concept that we apply to our transformation effort. This involves working diligently with the trends and signals that might affect us in our organization, when we ideate the possible solutions, explore and evaluate them, and uncover the plan for establishing the preferred solution.

Futures Thinking will apply to your change management effort, both in the Settlers and the Explorers situation. Regardless of your situation, the same approach is applicable:

- Identify your challenge, timeframe, ecosystem and the people you're working with. Document your transformational call to action
- Identify the trends and signals that might affect your scenarios and your plan to get there. Make sure to look for internal signals as well
- Diverge: Use Signal Sorting to understand the effects of the trends and signals, the Likelihood of impact, and the Likeability of the impact
- Converge: Identify possible, plausible and preferable scenarios
- Diverge: Explore and Evaluate the scenarios and the implementation plans via hypothesis-driven experiments
- Converge: Select your preferred scenario and implementation plan by strategizing from the future state
- Investigate the consequences for structures, cultures, governance and the business model in your business unit. This becomes your transformation design
- Act on it

Throughout the process, we pay special attention to the stories, anecdotes, attitudes, slang, jargon, jokes and sarcasm present in the organization and among the various participants and stakeholders. We want to surface the biases, beliefs and myths that exist. In doing so, we want to reveal, reframe and rethink them as we imagine the change, engage the people, and evolve the solution and path forward.

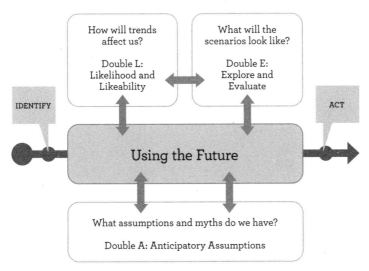

Figure 26
A simplified overview of the Using the Future
approach and process

These four primary components interact with each other throughout the process, as the learning in one area ripples into another. Using the Future is the spine of the approach, and consists of several principles, practices, workshops and tools, through which the other three components are initiated and refined.

Let's look at the process in detail.

DOUBLE L DOUBLE A DOUBLE E

Unpacking the process reveals that the approach is both linear and nonlinear, and sequential and iterative. And, the workshop components can to some extent be reordered to fit your situation, need, organizational inertia (either hunger or satiation, eagerness or reluctance, fast-paced or slow-paced), and learning through the progress.

Below I will show and describe a proven approach, which has been refined via **participatory action-learning with clients** from industries like life sciences, healthcare, software development, management consulting, engineering, product manufacturing and higher education. It has also been tested across functional domains like HR, People and Culture, Strategy, Organizational Design, Sales and Marketing, R&D and IT.

The model is partially based on this practical learning, and partly inspired by similar approaches, including but not limited to the Copenhagen Method, from Copenhagen Institute for Futures Studies, the methodology used in courses by Institute for the Future, the elements and tools described by Jan Oliver Schwarz,[60] and the Futures Literacy Lab.[61] You'll also see that that approach has analogies to Theory U: co-initiating, co-sensing, presencing, co-creating and co-evolving.[62]

Here is the detailed process for Using the Future in transformation and change management.

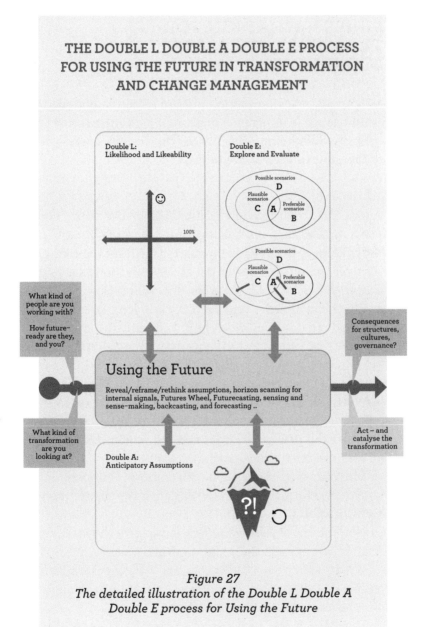

Figure 27
The detailed illustration of the Double L Double A
Double E process for Using the Future

PHASE 1: WHAT KIND OF TRANSFORMATION ARE YOU LOOKING AT?

As with any transformation or exploration, the first interest in change is initiated by necessity, force, inspiration or curiosity. Something either pushes you or pulls you toward change, toward alternative futures.

PUSH OR PULL?

You need to understand the direction of this force, and ascertain whether your colleagues see the situation differently. These initial, vital conversations will set the tone of voice for the rest of the phases, as they shed light on your diverse views on your situation and your willingness to investigate alternative futures. Some will long for the past, the good old days, and won't be able to rally the energy or attention necessary to challenge the present. Others are eager to embrace all the new stuff, technically, socially and structurally, and can't wait to get started. Maybe you feel paralysed, and unable to affect your future, hindered by organizational habits or myths. Or, you might feel optimistic about the new possibilities and the influence you have on your direction and your future.

These are crucial discussions that inform your planning for the transformation, and the design of the change management efforts.

How futures-ready are you? 'You' is used broadly here, as an identifier for you personally, your team and your organization.

What's your Temporal Anchoring? What's pushing and pulling you, or weighing you down in the Futures Triangle? (See the tools described in PART TWO.)

How VUCA is your world? And how BANI does it feel to you?

WHAT TRANSFORMATION ARE YOU LOOKING AT?

Some of you just want to extrapolate from where you are and plan for the Projected Future. This is the default extrapolated baseline, the business as usual future, as Voros described it.[63] Others want to deliberately create a divergent plan, and explore an alternative Preferred Future. And, some want to investigate the trends and movements, to see what emerges as you go along.

Are you a Settler into a specific future, or willing to Explore the futures?

What's your time horizon? A year? Two? Five or ten years?

And what's the size of your ecosystem? Is it your team, your business unit, your cross-functional program, or something else?

YOUR CALL TO ACTION DESCRIPTION

1: What's the situation in your organization?

2: What triggers your curiosity for an alternative future?

3: What pushes you toward an alternative future?

4: What pulls you toward an alternative future?

5: What can you gain from exploring the alternative futures?

6: What happens if you don't do anything?

7: What's your time horizon?

8: What's the size of your ecosystem? Who is part of it?

9: How futures-ready are you?

10: What is your level of VUCA and BANI?

THINGS TO DO IN PHASE 1

- Get familiar with Futures Literacy and Futures Thinking

- Reflect on your level of VUCA and BANI

- Reflect on how futures-ready you are, and your Temporal Anchoring/the Futures Triangle

- Describe the situation you're in, your time horizon for change, and the size of your ecosystem

- Describe why you want to change, and what pushes and pulls you toward alternative futures

PHASE 2: USING THE FUTURE

From here, a practical approach can be to split the work into three focus areas:

- A process part of **Using the Future**, focusing on tying it all together, rallying people, educating them in Futures Literacy, and ensuring that this is a participatory, action-learning approach
- An area focusing on collecting and sorting trends and signals (the **Double L**: Likelihood and Likeability), and on helping you and the organization explore and evaluate alternative futures (the **Double E**: Explore and Evaluate)
- The process of focusing on **Anticipatory Assumptions** (the Double A), on biases and beliefs, and on organizational myths

These three parts interact and inform each other with regard to content and form. Frequent adjustments and alignment between the participants are needed, as knowledge and learning emerge and people become increasingly futures literate.[64]

The best results are reached when the process is participatory and well facilitated,[65] and when the introduction to Futures Literacy and Futures Thinking is central and carefully crafted to the audience. Transparency and psychological safety are clearly key to having the most fruitful dialogues and achieving intended outcomes.

> The mastery of Anticipatory Leadership in individuals,
> and shared in the group, is a significant lever and
> catalyst for the emotional impact and the specific
> outcome of the Using the Future process.

See PART FOUR regarding Anticipatory Leadership and the emotional impact of this participatory, action-learning approach on involving people in exploring and evaluating their alternative futures — the benefits of involving people in understanding and designing the change.

THE PROCESS PART OF USING THE FUTURE

The goal with the Using the Future process is to focus on the union of the three circles in the Venn diagram depicted below.

**USING FUTURES THINKING AS
A VEHICLE FOR EXPLORING AND
EVALUATING THE INTERSECTION OF THE
FUTURE OF X AND YOUR ORGANIZATION**

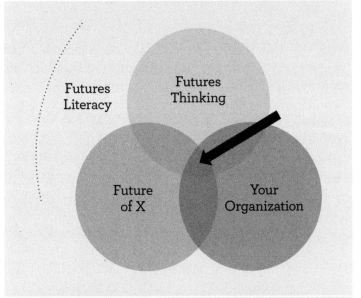

We use the mechanisms from Futures Thinking to explore how external and internal trends and signals affect you, and what scenarios emerge.

Throughout the process we keep an eye on the Anticipatory Assumptions in our organization.

After jointly understanding your transformational call to action, as created in Phase 1, a number of participatory, action-learning workshops should take place.

Design and execute a Futures Literacy Lab

- Train people in the ability and capacity to think critically and abstractly about the future
- Help them master how to reveal, reframe and rethink their Anticipatory Assumptions, their biases and beliefs, and the myths in the organization
- The theme/topic for the Futures Literacy Lab does not have to be connected to the problem at hand. The main goal is to understand what Futures Literacy is, how it works, why it works, and why you should engage in the future

Perform Horizon Scanning for trends and signals, externally and internally

- You need a pile of trends and signals to work with. This is the Magic Dust for your Futures Thinking process, which makes the generic process turn relevant and contextualized to you and your ecosystem.
- You're looking for trends and signals within the Future of X. You need to determine the aspects of X
  › X can be your industry, like life sciences, FMCG or banking
  › X can be your function, like HR, Finance or R&D
  › X can be the technology you're working with
  › X can be the ecosystem, society, community and customer base you work with
  › X can be one, several, or all of the above
- These trends and signals can be external or internal
  › Get hold of various publications, especially from the large consultancies, OECD, the World Economic Forum and similar organizations, specific signal databases, news media, newsletters and online forums. Listen to anecdotes from people and ask ChatGPT or another LLM for input.

See the earlier chapter on where to look and what to look for.

> Pay special attention to the internal signals: things you observe that make you go 'huh.' Things you sense and hear, that make you wonder. These internal trends and signals are of special importance to us in the ecosystem we're in, inside the organization.

• You might want to group and categorize the trends and signals for easy overview. You may also want to gently trim the list, to not get overwhelmed with too many elements. More than 15–20 trends and signals are too time-consuming in a workshop setting and might not increase the quality of the output. The Law of Diminishing Returns applies here.

• Finally, evaluate the perceived strength of the trend or signal, which can be characterized by its frequency, consistency, source credibility, velocity or peer validation.

TRENDS AND SIGNALS

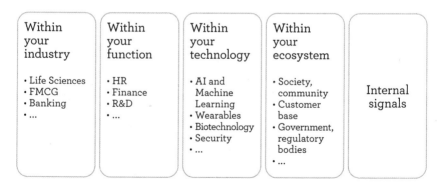

Figure 28
The different origins of trends and signals

You might want to gather your signals in a so-called signal radar. Here is an example of such a signal scanning effort.

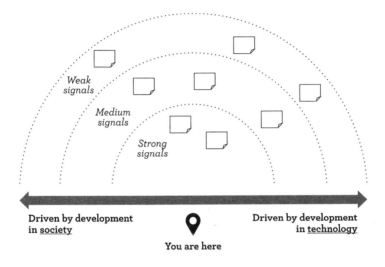

Figure 29
Example of a signal radar

Perform your Signal Sorting workshop
- This is the Double L: Likelihood and Likeability
- For each of the trends and signals that you just identified, ask yourself this:
  › What is the bias of the source of the trend?
  › What is the likelihood of this trend affecting us, in our ecosystem? What is the probability that this will affect us?
  › What is the likeability of the effect this trend has for us? Do we like the effect it has?
- During this workshop, have a designated person to listen for biases, beliefs and myths, as well as Anticipatory Assumptions. Make a list of those.

REFLECTING ON YOUR ABILITY TO INFLUENCE THE EFFECT OF THE TRENDS

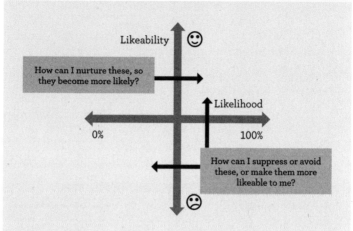

Ask yourself:

For those trends and signals with low likelihood and high likeability:

I really like them, so how can I nurture them so that they increase their likelihood? Or, what will affect the likeability negatively?

For the trends and signals with low likeability and high likelihood:

I don't like them, so how can I decrease their likelihood? Or, change my point of view on their likeability?

Now is a good time to revisit the survey on futures-readiness, and consider:
- How much will things change?
- How worried or optimistic are you?
- How much influence do you have?

Deep dive into the effects and consequences of those trends and signals that 'jump out' or demand further attention

- Have a Futures Wheel workshop on those trends and signals that you need to explore further
- Uncover first-, second- and third-order impacts. Describe in detail how that trend or signal unfolds and what ripple effects it has
- Reflect on whether that changes the placement in the Signal-Sorting cross. Has your perception of likelihood or likeability changed?
- Capture the assumptions and myths that are uncovered and emerge during the session

Futurecasting: Establish the possible scenarios

- Now, zoom in on a few possible scenarios for your transformation or change activity, considering: (a) Your call to action description from Phase 1; (b) The Signal Sorting and the Futures Wheel workshops from above
- Create plausible scenarios, preferable scenarios and perfect scenarios. Maybe you also want to create a scenario that you find unattractive. These groups of scenarios might not overlap. Generally speaking, 3–5 scenarios would be a manageable number of alternative futures to work with
- Explore them. Draw and describe them. Sketch artefacts and compose short stories and mocked-up postcards, news articles, podcast episodes or videos from the scenarios. Build them in LEGO. Simulate the scenarios or futures with role-playing. This is called 'Standing in the Future'
- Give all the details to your favourite LLM and explore it further with questions, asking for opposing points of view and blind spots. Be aware of the limitations of such an approach

145

- Use this information and your personal, emotional responses to the futures to adjust the placement of your scenarios in your scenario map
- Document the assumptions and myths that arise during the session

FUTURECASTING: SCENARIOS, AND THEIR PLACEMENT IN THE SCENARIO MAP

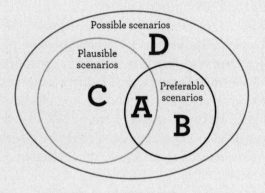

Create plausible, preferable and perfect scenarios. These groups of scenarios might not overlap. A short list of 3-5 scenarios is a manageable number of alternative futures to work with.

Explore them. Thoroughly.

Capture your emotional responses to the scenarios.

Adjust the placement of the scenarios in the map with that learning in mind.

Backcasting — imagine the path to the future

- Now you need to calculate backwards from the future
- Pick the future or scenario that you want to work with. A logical choice will be a scenario that is both plausible and preferable, but you can also select a non-plausible, non-preferable scenario to investigate the path to that, as a pre-mortem exercise
- Now we time-travel backwards, from that future that takes place, say, five years from now
- Imagine that you're only one year from that future. What needs to happen and what needs to be in place for that future to emerge?
- Imagine now that you are three years from that future. What needs to be done then?
- And then, imagine that you are five years from that future. What needs to be done now, for those other actions and elements to work?
- This gives you a backwards roadmap, from which you can devise a forward-looking plan and a forecast for your activities, the necessary investments (time and money), and your transformation and change
- Again, make note of the assumptions and myths that come up in the session

Jointly, the process could look like this:

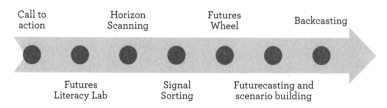

Figure 30
An example of the sequence of workshops
and tools in a Futures Thinking process

THE OUTCOMES FROM USING
THE FUTURE PROCESS

From the process, several concrete outcomes appear. The scenarios and the path forward are the tangible ones, feeding directly into the transformation process.

The list of myths and Anticipatory Assumptions will serve as guidelines for the involvement of employees and stakeholders in the transformation. These myths and assumptions can be confirmed or busted, challenged, tested, verified or refuted ... as well as eliminated, lubricated or merely accepted. Either way, they feed into the engagement and mobilization activities in the transformation and change process.

More importantly, a significant outcome from the process is educational and emotional.

First, the Using the Future process increases your Futures Literacy. You increase your awareness of trends and signals, imagine how they unfold, know how to use the future, and know why.

Second, you gain insight into your own and each other's points of view, assumptions and myths. You reveal, reframe and rethink them, and learn together.

Third, it strengthens your Anticipatory Leadership. You sharpen your ability to be curious, listen, sense, sense-make, imagine, master storytelling, be open-minded, be playful and have mental flexibility.

Finally, the process creates hope, ownership and confidence in the way forward.

I am so amazed — in awe, really — every time we run these processes, with countless variations, and these emotions of hope, ownership and confidence slowly but steadily emerge.

In PART FOUR, we deep-dive into the Anticipatory Leadership and the emotions that an engaged Futures Thinking process evokes.

THINGS TO DO IN PHASE 2

- Conduct a Futures Literacy Lab

- Perform Horizon Scanning, looking for external and internal signals

- Pay extra attention to the internal signals

- Host a Signal Sorting workshop, and a Futures Wheel workshop

- Perform the Futurecasting and design the scenarios

- Do the Backcasting and roadmapping work

- Look for assumptions and myths, and create a Myth Log

PHASE 3: SKETCHING YOUR TRANSFORMATION AND CHANGE PROCESS

Now you have two options for planning and enabling your transformation: as Settler or as Explorer.

The Settler knows where to go, marks the spot on the map, plans and executes accordingly. The Settler has identified the scenario and the future that's preferable for them, but still keeps an eye out for findings and learnings in the process.

The Explorer is still looking for the right place to go, and keeps exploring and evaluating the places and the plans. The Explorer might have a preferred scenario, but embraces the multiplicity of alternative scenarios and futures. In their quest, they deliberately set up experiments to evaluate the scenarios, so they can update their scenario map.

I know I'm making this starkly black and white, and rather unnuanced, and I hope you bear with me here. This is simply to illustrate two different approaches to tackling the VUCA/BANI world that leaders describe:

In a volatile, uncertain, complex world with ambiguous answers to questions, we need to be adaptable to change (VUCA).

By doing that properly, we strive to mitigate the feeling of a brittle world, of anxiety, of nonlinearity, and of incomprehensibility (BANI).

The Settler does that by having built-in learning loops in the process. You involve people, plan toward the scenario, translate to context, embrace, reflect and adjust. The Settler has one single scenario and handles the VUCAness toward that scenario in the implementation. This single loop/double loop learning process is thoroughly described in other professional literature.

The Explorer, on the other hand, does that by having a scenario-based, hypothesis-driven experimental approach to exploring and evaluating the alternative futures. This is where we use the Double E element once again.

A scenario-based, hypothesis-driven experimental approach
During the Using the Future process you have identified scenarios with a perceived degree of predictability and desirability. These characteristics have been assigned to the scenarios through your Signal Sorting, using the Double L element (Likelihood and Likeability) on the signals, and by the Futurecasting process of building the scenarios. During these processes you have revealed, reframed and rethought your assumptions, and discussed your myths.

Now you stand with a few alternative futures in your scenario map.

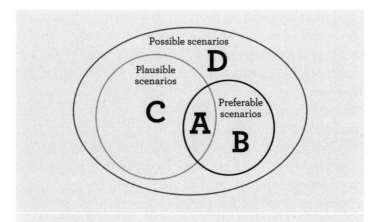

In this map, scenario A is both plausible and preferable.

B is preferable, but not plausible.
C is not preferable, but plausible.
D is neither preferable, nor plausible.

But how can you qualify this further? And how can you eliminate scenarios from your list?

One approach is to establish and conduct hypothesis-driven experiments to learn more about the characteristics of the scenarios. These hypotheses can relate to the scenario itself, to the way to establish the scenario, to the organizational assumptions and myths, or to the prerequisites for success.

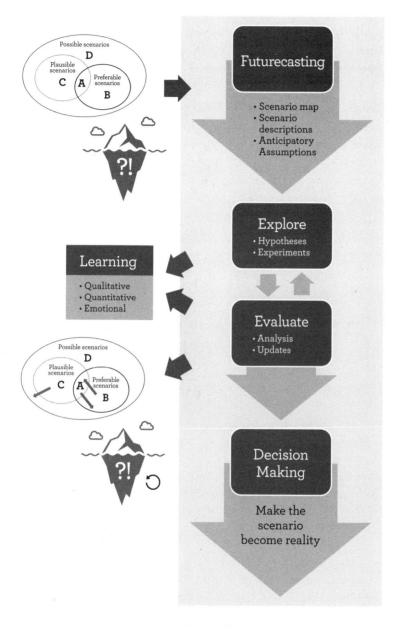

Figure 31
The Explore-and-evaluate process

In the start-up world, many entrepreneurs do this by the Build-Measure-Learn approach, as described by entrepreneur Eric Ries in his great book, *The Lean Startup*.[67]

In the world of business innovation, people might prefer the framework Alexander Osterwalder and David J. Bland provided in their book, *Testing Business Ideas: A Field Guide for Rapid Experimentation*.[68]

In both cases, and in our approach, the hypotheses are used to qualify the scenarios at hand via real-life experiments. This carries the Futurecasting from 'the lab' into the organization, to harvest learning together with employees and stakeholders.

One way to describe the experiments is to be inspired by Osterwalder's and Bland's test cards and learning cards:

TEST CARD	LEARNING CARD
Step 1: Hypothesis We believe that:	Step 1: Hypothesis We believed that:
Step 2: Test To verify that, we will:	Step 2: Observation We observed:
Step 3: Metric And measure:	Step 3: Learnings and insights From that, we learned that:
Step 4: Criteria We are right if:	Step 4: Decisions and actions Therefore, we will:

The data you collect can be quantitative, qualitative or emotional, and lead you to evaluate the scenario:

- How does it change the scenario map?
  How does it change the probability?
  How does it change the desirability?
- What do we need to update in the scenario if we want to make it more desirable, or have a higher probability?
- How does it change the plan to get there?
  What do we need to take into consideration?
- How does it change our business model (what we do)?
- How does it change our structures, cultures and governance (how we do it)?
- And, as usual, what insights does it provide into our Anticipatory Assumptions, and the organizational myths?

THE HYPOTHESIS-DRIVEN EXPERIMENTS MIGHT LEAD TO AN UPDATE OF BOTH THE SCENARIO MAP AND THE LIST OF ANTICIPATORY ASSUMPTIONS

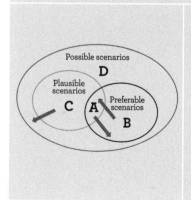

Anticipatory Assumptions

During these experiments we gradually qualify our scenarios and plans to establish them and eliminate those that are less preferable.

From here, a more classic transformation process starts.

THINGS TO DO IN PHASE 3

- Explore and evaluate the scenarios via hypotheses and experiments

- Update the scenario map, the Anticipatory Assumptions and your Myth Log

- Investigate the effects this has on the structures, cultures, governance and business model

---

What is missing now is: (1) How to look for signals inside your organization; (2) How to challenge and revisit the assumptions, which you build your view of the future on; (3) How to use this understanding of trends and signals in society and technology to design your organization, culture and governance.

Let's unpack those topics.

TRENDS AND SIGNALS, SENSED AND RECEIVED
BY TIMM URSCHINGER
Transformation Architect at EY,
Co-Creator of Teal Around The World

Location: Central Europe

- AI/Technology is seen as a salvation
  (which I think won't do the job)

- Profits over commitments to ESG
  (Environmental, Social and Governance)
  and SDG (Sustainable Development Goals)

- Business Transformation rather than only
  Product/Market Innovation

- Busting bureaucracy as focus for organizations

- Focus on humans over systems

- Healthy life focus

- Back to nature and local communities

- Narrative of 'more' being challenged

- Uproar against authorities

- Do-gooder vs. real acts of defiance

- Being alone while being always connected

- Networks of leaders rather than 'a' leader

The signals are grouped but not ranked. Note that some
of these are directly counteracting and paradoxical.

SIGNALS INSIDE MY ORGANIZATION

Trends and signals are the Magic Dust, the super ingredient, of the Futures Thinking process. Those signals, put in context of your organization, are what makes the rather generic process of Futures Thinking relevant to you.

Previously, we described the trends and signals like this:

Term	Short description
Megatrend	A large, transformative trend with global impact and long duration, stable even in turbulent times. These are typically almost irreversible.
Trend	A general direction of change over time, identifiable in societal, technological, economic, environmental and political (STEEP) domains.
Signal	Concrete, observable evidence in the present that hints at future trends, such as anormal events, new technologies or surprising policies.
Driver	Underlying forces that shape future trends, including broad, long-term phenomena like climate change or demographic shifts.
Wild Card	Low-probability, high-impact events that are unpredictable but can dramatically change the future landscape.
Black Swan	Rare, high-impact events that are unexpected and hard to predict, with explanations that make them seem predictable in hindsight.

**The terms with the highest degree of
usefulness to us are trends and signals,**
as they affect us at a level of magnitude where
we can act, react, counteract or non-act on the
impact this development might have.

Trends and signals are within our
'circle of influence,' our ecosystem.

Additionally, during the discussion of the Horizon Scanning process, we identified several sources of trends and signals, including **internal** signals. Since we are applying the philosophies, principles, mechanisms and tools of Strategic Foresight and Futures Thinking to the **inside** of the organization, the time horizon, ecosystem, involved people and sources of the trends and signals shift to the **inside**, as described earlier.

Thus, in addition to our curiosity about external trends and signals, we are interested in those movements that take place inside the organization, as they might snowball and affect us sooner or later.

**Internal signals are anomalies inside
our organization.**

They are subtle cues that provide insight into
potential trends and emerging changes.

These signals can come from various people,
groups, teams and functions, and can be identified
via employee feedback, observations in behavioural
change, shifts in team dynamics, new perceptions
of the culture, and in other ways.

Scanning for internal signals should be a regular,
recurring practice in your team.

Sensing the organizational movements is
a competency of Anticipatory Leadership.

Signals are real. They are not rumours or hearsay, but real examples of new and anormal things, emotions or perceptions that emerge in the organization. They can be plentiful, strong, weak or few and far between, but they are real.

THE SOURCES THAT FEED INTO YOUR
SIGNAL DATABASE

In the organization, you have several ways of picking up, intercepting, receiving and collecting signals.

- You can develop and master the skill of picking up the signals yourself
- Your team can develop a habit of collecting and sharing the signals they pick up

- Your organization can get in the habit of sharing their observations with you
- You can establish a network of so-called Trend Receivers

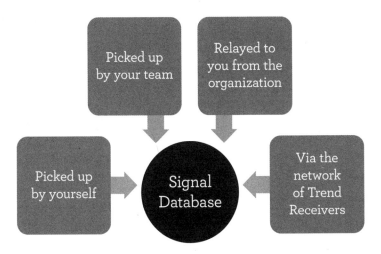

Figure 32
Gathering input for your Signal Database

Rupert Hofmann from Audi Business Innovation has described these Trend Receivers:

"**Trend receivers** are individuals who perceive changes and potentials of the new in a specific domain in a highly sensitive and differentiated way. They have connections in many contexts and have discerning views of what drives people and what aspects are undergoing change. The ability to imagine and project respectively their visionary competence results from a combination of characteristics: everyday experience in a certain context (in the consumer arena, with a given product or service), curiosity, open-mindedness, the ability to observe and recognize patterns, life experience, network, and intuition."[69]

Throughout this book you will find reports from people I value as Trend Receivers from the US, Europe and Asia Pacific, sharing what they see and sense. They are examples of both signals and Trend Receivers: People who are good at sensing, intercepting and picking up the vague and anormal cues that indicate that a signal is present.

They jointly add to, augment and refine a Signal Database. Each of the entries has a source, a context and a description of the movement they sense. These entries can also have metadata, like a perceived frequency, strength and momentum, and occasionally a personal perspective on the desirability of the effect.

Additionally, we can aggregate the entries and look for patterns and recognizable similarities. This can be done by scrutinizing the texts by hand or, if you have a vast amount of data, by feeding it into an LLM and asking for a summary. In our case, the volume of the data is manageable, and there is no need for AI here.

Despite the differences in geography, industry domain and functional affinity, these patterns seem to emerge related to work:

- A human and people-centric approach to work. There is focus on well-being, authenticity and meaningfulness. The DEI agenda is driven by the employees

- This contrasts with a lurking shift in leadership toward tangible, measurable goals, clear guidelines and boundaries, and connecting people with strategy

- There is a focus on execution, results and getting things done. The clock-speed of the organizations is increasing

- Technology, especially AI, is seen as both a solution AND a source of concern

- Some signals point toward a stronger embrace of New Ways of Working, while others point to the exact opposite

It seems like a paradoxical development that includes opposing forces. The question is how individual business units and organizations perceive them — and support or suppress them.

WHAT TO LOOK FOR
– EXAMPLES OF INTERNAL ANOMALIES

Signals emerge as anomalies. They might manifest as unusual behaviour (or happenings, opinions or statements), that can reveal the beginning of an abnormal movement inside your organization. And, they might be weak or vague.

When paying attention to this, over time you will sharpen the skill and almost unconsciously pick up on the signals and bring them to the table. To help with this, establish a network of trend receivers in your organization, reach out to the cultural zealots in your ecosystem and lurking in the crazy, progressive teams. Surely, they have stories to tell and signals to share.

Here is a **short list of selected approaches** I use for listening for signals among the organizations I'm in contact with.

They are things I look for, places where I search and people I talk to:

- Surprising 'Communities of Interest' in your organization
  > What book clubs do you have that surprise you? What nerdy, geeky communities exist? These gatherings might reveal a thirst for finding like-minded people that the organization doesn't foster. They might also reveal an interest in new and emerging technologies or movements that currently live at the grassroots level but could be nurtured for the benefit of more people and the organization as a whole.
  > Example: In a life sciences organization, a network formed around studying psychological safety, accountability and the willingness to distribute power, hinting at an unmet need related to training and acceptance.
  > Example: In an HR department, a show-and-tell session about the use of AI for writing annual appraisal feedback was held, despite an explicit company ban on AI for this. To the leaders in the organization, these annual feedback tasks were notorious for being dreadfully time consuming, and HR wanted to be on top of the challenge.
- Unusual requests for training
  > Which courses are asked for that are not part of the strategy? These requests reveal unmet needs, and could uncover activities in the organization that are not part of the strategy. This might lead to revising the strategy and changing course.
  > Example: In a life sciences organization, requests for training in Chinese revealed promising marketing and sales activity in Asia, despite the strategic choice not to enter that market yet.

> › Example: In a global finance department, training and peer-to-peer networking were established around organizational change management, a topic traditionally not anchored in that department.

- Eyebrow-raising comments in employee feedback forms
  > › Paying attention to comments in employee feedback will reveal unarticulated voices and rebellious behaviour. These remarks sometimes serve as a steam valve for mental pressure building in the organization.
  > › Example: In a bank, an employee asked for more 'drunk coding,' in the very literal sense. She proposed having group sessions with pizza and beer, to prompt more creative, bold energy in their programming and solutioning.

- Changed tone of voice in job posting
  > › A new tone of voice in public or internal job postings is a signal about a change either in the recruitment process, in the business unit that is hiring, or as a larger company policy.
  > › Example: In a life sciences organization, using terminology from the world of New Ways of Working was a strong signal that: (a) The team worked differently than their peer teams; (b) They want to appeal to a new demographic group.
  > › Example: In public and private organizations in Denmark, an effort is made to remove masculine language and make job postings gender neutral, to attract a more diverse group of applicants.

- Changed vocabulary in meetings or Town Hall sessions.
  > › Listening for a change in the balance of competitive, direct and 'getting things done' language, versus inclusive, sensing and reflecting language,

> can reveal a changed mindset or approach to communication and dialogue, and a shift in culture in the team or organization.

> › Example: In a leadership team in a green tech/ engineering organization, there was a shift from primarily direct language to what appeared to be a 50/50 balance between that and a more sensing style. This revealed an emerging shift in the culture, spearheading a companywide change toward a more inclusive, involving approach over the next 2–3 years.

You can also detect signals by looking for emerging changes in search words or searching patterns in MS Teams, Google Workspace or similar companywide productivity tools. This is a sensitive topic that raises privacy and surveillance concerns. However, I know of a few organizations that regularly look through employee search histories with data that is made anonymous, hoping to spot new or surprising queries.

In general, you're looking for behaviour that is unusual, surprises you, and is the possible first sign of an emerging sentiment that might snowball into a disruptive change in the organization.

The more aware you are of these anomalies and signals, the more you start picking them up and intercepting them. And, you get better at collaborating with your team and Trend Receivers inside the organization, providing a holistic view of shifts and changes in your ecosystem.

What you are doing here is performing **Horizon Scanning** to spot movements that are far away.

Stand on your toes, climb onto a chair or a ladder to broaden your perspective, and engage other horizon scanners in your curiosity to get more perspectives, points of view and observations.

WHAT TO DO ABOUT THEM
– FROM OBSERVATIONS TO SIGNALS

With the list of observations and anomalies, a bit of work is needed to uncover and understand the thoughts, request, movement or **driver that the behaviour is representation of**. This anomaly is merely an instantiation of the underlying force, so you need to investigate it.

First, interview the source of the information. Uncover the hidden or unvoiced request or need for change that the observation represents. These observations hide, and can reveal, a signal of change: Concrete, observable evidence in the present that hints at future trends, such as anormal events, new technologies or surprising policies.

Second, with that understanding in hand, drop it into the Futures Wheel to investigate the possible ripple effects of the signal. 'If *this* signal happens on large scale, then *that* happens as a result.' Unfold the second-order consequences too, as well as the third-order consequences.

Third, ask yourself what it takes to nurture this signal, so it becomes a trend in the organization. You need to understand the premise for growth and acceptance in the culture, as part of your investigation of the nature of the signal.

Fourth, imagine that the signal gets firmly rooted and gains traction in the organization. Familiarize yourself with that alternative future, where this signal has become a reality. Capture your emotional response to that scenario.

Fifth, place the signal in your signal cross: How likely is it that this signal affects us? Do you like the effect it will have?

Finally, clarify whether you want to accept, embrace, ignore, support or even suppress this signal.

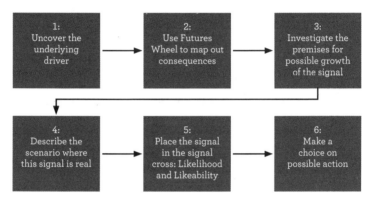

Figure 33
Working with the myths, observations
and organizational assumptions

The trends and signals, from both external and internal sources, are the Magic Dust in your Futures Thinking approach. Putting the trends and signals into the context of your organization makes it possible for you to futurecast and describe possible, alternative futures, taking internal cultural movements into account.

In the case of a transformation (a significant and intentional change in the structure, culture, governance, processes or strategies of an organization), the internal signals play a vital role as taletellers, sources of information and hints of possible friction or emerging forces that we need to embrace. They can help us Use the Future by engaging and acknowledging the people in the organization.

UNCOVERING AND MANAGING ANTICIPATORY ASSUMPTIONS INSIDE YOUR ORGANIZATION

Whether deliberately or inadvertently, throughout the Futures Thinking process and via the mechanisms and workshops we have uncovered the so-called Anticipatory Assumptions. Recall that anticipation and assumptions are building blocks in Futures Literacy.

"The future does not exist in the present but anticipation does.
The form the future takes in the present is anticipation."
— Riel Miller

One role of the Futures Literacy Lab is to reveal, reframe and rethink the Anticipatory Assumptions, as these support us in uncovering, discussing and considering the cultural stories, myths, values, biases and beliefs. They shape our behaviour, engagement, authenticity and change-readiness.

Remember the three questions regarding the Future Outlook, as described by Jane McGonigal:[70]

- How much will things change in the next years?
- How worried or optimistic are you?
- How much influence do you have?

The answers will help you in understanding the approach to alternative futures in your ecosystem and organization.

Listening to the vocalized and the tacit assumptions about the future in your organization is an extremely valuable source of information for your transformation project. They reveal the culture, and the personal stance toward the change.

THE CULTURAL ICEBERG
IN YOUR ORGANIZATION

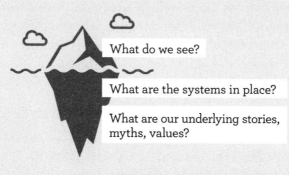

What do we see?

What are the systems in place?

What are our underlying stories,
myths, values?

Figure 34
A version of the classical cultural iceberg

An iceberg has long been used as a symbolic metaphor
for how only a small portion of something — for
instance, an organizational culture — is visible, while
the rest is hidden.

To understand the deeper aspects of the culture, like
biases, beliefs and myths, we need to pay attention to
what 'goes on below the surface.'

We can take advantage of that knowledge for our
transformation, related to: (a) The nature, probability
and desirability of the scenarios we imagine; (b) The
resistance and reluctance to change; (c) The approaches
to mobilize the people we engage with.

The idea of illustrating and discussing culture as an iceberg with visible and hidden parts has its critics, who suggest it's a naïve oversimplification. Otti Vogt, Co-Founder at Good Organisations, has said, "It's time to shift the conversation from simplistic, individualistic and linear change models to a more systemic view that recognizes the complex nature of organizational behaviour."[71] A more comprehensive methodology would be to apply the approaches from cybernetics[72] and systems thinking to capture and acknowledge the complexity of the organization and of change. The point would be to highlight the interdependency between structures, cultures and people, also focusing on the feedback-and-control mechanisms in official and tacit governance.

Regardless of whether you look at it in terms of the linear, iceberg model or the nonlinear, multidimensional systems thinking model, organizational and personal Anticipatory Assumptions play a vital role in Futurecasting of the transformation. The outcomes from applying Futures Thinking to the inside of the organization when imagining possible scenarios and alternative futures will indisputably be affected by the myths, biases, beliefs and values. Used diligently, the Futures Thinking approach helps us reveal these.

Anticipatory Assumptions can help in envisioning possible future scenarios and evaluating trends and signals, and they can shape the foundation upon which possible, plausible and preferable futures are built.

Biases, beliefs and myths can lead to distorted views of the future if not addressed and accounted for. They can influence one's perspective on what is desirable or possible in the future.

Here are a few real examples of assumptions and organizational myths that I've picked up in my work with Futures Thinking and transformations in organizations:

- 100% allocation to projects is never going to happen
- The annual budget process always takes place in Q3
- Our growth will continue for the next five years
- We will always have the annual appraisal process
- There will always be titles and a title hierarchy
- My job will not be replaced by AI
- My job will absolutely be replaced by AI
- The strategy team is a bunch of blue-eyed optimists
- Top management has no idea about the real problems
- The people in the organization have no idea about the real problems
- Every team would love self-management
- Trust in the organization is a one-way street
- Fear is dominating the decision-making process
- Agile and Scrum will be rolled out across the organization, from the top
- We are too busy to have time to think
- The future direction is given by top management; we cannot change it
- The older generation are slow learners
- The younger generation are lazy workers
- Work From Home makes people underperform
- The DEI agenda is not taken seriously by middle management
- 2024 is the year of execution

Note that these examples are a mix of assumptions and myths, opinions, rumours and hearsay. It can be difficult to categorize them and qualify whether a statement is an informed prediction based on experience and data, or an idea formed by cultural or personal narratives.

WORKING WITH THE ASSUMPTIONS AND MYTHS

My empirical hypothesis from the action-learning processes of Futures Thinking is that **a strict discernment** between Anticipatory Assumptions as described by Miller[73] and Bergheim,[74] and the crude bulk of opinions and myths, is **not always immensely useful** in the operational, hands-on processes employed in Futures Thinking/Using the Future-workshops. They can for the most part be treated similarly in the engagement and design processes.

It is, however, valuable to distinguish between those that are personal and those that are organizational, to understand how widespread and how sticky the opinion, bias, belief, myth or assumption is. Is it only a few people who have this point of view, or is it an organizational, cultural, habitual or leadership-based assumption?

> Assumptions and myths will inform, shape
> and distort the images and stories that we tell
> ourselves about the characteristics of the futures,
> and about the probability and desirability
> of such futures.

Some assumptions and myths are shaped by organizational information, and can thus be challenged, tested, verified or refuted. Similarly, some beliefs or ideas that are accepted as true without proof can undergo scrutiny to determine their validity. In these cases, where we can compile data or collect truths, we can verify or refute the assumption or myth.

Other assumptions and myths are personal beliefs, grounded in Temporal Anchoring, shaped by their history and by decades of business experience, and by behavioural training in the organizations. These are much harder to embrace, change and develop, as they are firmly rooted in the individual's mind, thoughts and behavioural habits.

In all cases, **the task with assumptions and myths is to reveal, reframe and rethink them**. Obviously, this exercise is at the core of the Futures Literacy Labs, and serves as the vehicle for developing your futures literacy. But, in the Futures Thinking process it helps us understand and embrace the mental premise for the mindset of the people who are involved in exploring and evaluating the possible, alternative futures in the transformation. This will in turn affect engagement, ownership and confidence in the future, and will shape change-enablement actions and efficiency.

For each of these assumptions and myths, you should investigate how to change the conditions for change.

CHANGING THE CONDITIONS FOR CHANGE

Anticipatory Assumptions

For each Anticipatiory Assumption, belief, bias and myth:

Uncover:
- What is the origin? Where and who does it come from? What triggers or nurses it?
- Is it based on information and data, or on unverified perceptions and narratives?
- Can it be immediately refuted, busted or falsified?
- What is the likely future if this assumption and myth unfolds?
- What do you think is going to happen if your assumption is correct?
- What future would you like to see happening instead?

Change the conditions for change:
- How difficult is it to rethink the assumption?
- How can we change the conditions for change?

As described in PART TWO, regarding the mechanisms in the Futures Thinking process, several tools can support you and your organization in a comfortable, open and beneficial learning session regarding the scenarios. There, we can harvest and document the assumptions and myths:

- Signal Sorting reveals assumptions
- The Futures Wheel reveals assumptions
- The classic Five Why's process works too
- A Fish Bone diagram traces root causes and helps reveal and bust myths
- The Assumption Mapping tool from project management is a classic resource

A fun team exercise is to ask ChatGPT for a Futures Wheel, and then react to the findings.

Here is a prompt to start with:

Let's talk about Futures Thinking, signals and trends, and in particular the 'Futures Wheel' tool. Please create a Futures Wheel with four sub-branches. For each sub-branch, write the underlying assumption and the possible consequence. Give the sub-branches numbers, starting with 1.

The trend that you are looking at is: 'Employees are more interested in a hybrid work model, which combines working from an office and from home, than management is.'

THE EFFECT OF WORKING WITH ANTICIPATORY ASSUMPTIONS IN YOUR TRANSFORMATION

Apart from concrete updates to the list of myths, working with Anticipatory Assumptions in your transformation increases the quality of the scenarios and the validity of the evaluations of predictability and desirability.

The scenarios are better, the placement in the scenario map is more credible, the Backcasting and Forecasting are more realistic, and the mobilization of people is more efficient.

And what's more, the emotional impact is real: hope, ownership, confidence and agency.

TRENDS AND SIGNALS, SENSED AND RECEIVED
BY KASPER RISBJERG
Head of Venturing
Group Strategy, Development & Innovation
Ingka Group — IKEA

Location: Denmark, with a global footprint

Regarding what we do:
- Absolutely no sign of stepping away from a focus on ESG

- A shift in investment strategy from smaller ventures to larger ventures

- Immaterialization of the offer-to-market. Extension to services in the home, that is not only furniture and interior design. 'Those who own the relationship with the customer own the market.'

Regarding how we do it:
- Be greedy when others are fearful. Our strong brand and financial position allow us to take chances others cannot, and double-down when good opportunities come that fit our long-term strategy.

- Keep nurturing a culture of rapid experimentation and let teams work autonomously.

PART THREE AND A HALF:

THE DESIGN OF THE FUTURES-READY ORGANIZATION

Finally, we arrive at the last part of the transformation sketch process: What are the consequences of the Using the Future approach for your organizational design?

In this chapter, we look specifically at the first of the four questions that this book set out to answer:

> **How do I use my understanding of trends and signals in society and technology to design my organization, culture and governance?**

One useful approach will be to examine the futures and scenarios that emerged via the Using the Future processes, to help design the organizational structures, governance and cultures associated with those specific potential futures.

Typically, this kind of transformation is initiated, executed and driven by a leadership team or a group of transformational agents who lead this intense work on behalf of the business unit. Proper involvement of change agents, employees and stakeholders in the ecosystem is the professional approach to making this a joint effort and tapping into the collective intelligence of calculating the organizational consequences of the Explore-and-Evaluate phase.

Together, you sketch the organizational structure, considering the balance between hierarchy and self-leadership, renegotiating the decision mandate and distributed leadership, and discussing the enablement of local cultural dialects. You experiment with new technology and a possibly updated business model, pulling the customers (internally or externally) in the loop. You backcast together and design a Forecasting roadmap with familiar actions and experiments, thereby also engaging you and the organization in learning, picking up serendipitous information and emotional experiences, and constantly adjusting the design and approach. This works, and we will unpack it in the pages ahead.

THE LONG-TERM ORGANIZATIONAL TRANSFORMATION

Another approach that's more long term, permanent, fundamentally groundbreaking and genuinely disruptive is to equip and motivate the organization to infuse Using the Future into their habits. To make Horizon Scanning, Signal Sorting and Futures Wheels a part of their routines. To create a culture where it is natural and encouraged to surface, share and discuss assumptions, beliefs and myths regarding the present and the futures. To let the organization initiate the exploration and evaluation of plausible and preferable scenarios for how their future could look, putting them in the driver's seat. To activate the agency in the organization, without leadership prompting them and serving as a formal sponsor for the initiatives.

Surely, the first approach is a catalyst for the second, and we'll give diligent attention to the concrete methodology in the following chapters. The methods sketched out below could easily become part of the organizational cultural paradigm over time, driven by and embraced by the people, from the grassroots, and not solely led by a designated tactical foresight/transformation team (as it typically is).

This kind of approach has a number of characteristics that are different from what mindfulness coach Frederic Laloux has termed the classic, reactive 'orange' organizations in the business world:

- They **sense** what is going on around them, intercepting signals inside the organization and outside the ecosystem

- They use that information and the emotional reactions to proactively **take initiative** to embrace new things or mitigate and soothe the effect of unwanted trends
- They **playfully experiment** with ideas and concepts
- They **voluntarily shape-shift themselves** to fit the wants and needs of employees and stakeholders regarding structure, decision-making mechanisms, collaboration paradigms, and cultural virtues and norms
- They do not sit and wait for permission, but voluntarily **participate** in listening, analysing, exploring, evaluating and shaping their own ways of working
- They have **collective agency**

This can be characterized as **The Participatory Organization**, and it fits perfectly with the Anticipatory Leadership style and attributes we investigate in this book.

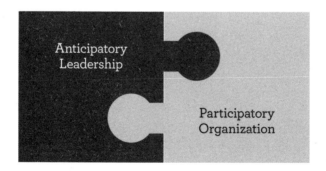

Figure 35
The Anticipatory Leadership and the Participatory
Organization fit together and can integrate well

The Participatory Organization that integrates Anticipatory Leadership is futures-ready. Organizations that master this integration enable a powerful combination of foresight and inclusivity that can significantly enhance an organization's ability to navigate future challenges while maintaining a strong and participatory internal culture. They become futures-ready by identifying and exploring future trends and changes, activating collective intelligence, initiating change based on Futurecasting, and inviting all people to participate in the evaluation and decision-making processes.

Participatory Organizations, with their inclusive approach, help ensure that transformations are designed in a way that considers the perspectives and needs of various stakeholders. This can make transformation and change management processes smoother and more effective, as employees are more likely to support changes they've had a hand in shaping. In this way, we enable agency.

THE TYPICAL BUILDING BLOCKS OF
THE PARTICIPATORY ORGANIZATION

We earlier described Sociocracy, Holacracy, Teal, Agile, Scrum and Humanocracy as some of the most prominent organizational methodologies and paradigms under the New Ways of Working umbrella.

If we characterize them according to their Anticipatory and Participatory nature, it could look like this:

Methodology	Anticipatory nature	Characteristics that support the Anticipatory capabilities	Participatory nature	Characteristics that support the Participatory capabilities
Teal	High	Self-management, evolutionary purpose, enabling continuous adaptation	High	Wholeness, decentralized decision-making, collective goal-setting, flat hierarchy
Holacracy	High	Distributed authority, rapid iteration, adaptability	Moderate	Roles over job titles, governance through collective decision-making, iterative governance meetings
Sociocracy	Moderate	Democratic participation, thorough and inclusive planning	High	Circular organizational structure, consent-based decision-making, linked teams
Agile	Moderate	Adaptability, iterative processes, operational adjustments	High	Teamwork, customer collaboration, responsiveness to change
Scrum	Moderate	Iterative processes, flexibility, frequent adjustments	Moderate	Sprint planning, daily standups, sprint reviews, team inputs
Humanocracy	High	Meritocracy of ideas, innovation, entrepreneurial mindset	High	Empowerment, entrepreneurial behaviour, dismantling hierarchies, busting bureaucracy

Clearly, the well-known methodologies for New Ways of Working are suitable for Participatory activities, as they are inherently designed to be so. In addition, they support the Anticipatory capabilities, thereby showing that:

**The futures-ready organization
is one that is designed with ...**

a) Those methodologies that embrace human-focused culture, inclusion, iteration and reflection
b) An organizational platform that serves as the scaffolding for more self-governed, and thus adaptable, teams
c) Futures Literacy as an organizational capability
d) Futures Thinking processes built naturally into their scanning, reflection and evaluation mechanisms

---

So, organizations that are already using New Ways of Working and designing themselves accordingly have the potential to easily adopt Anticipatory Leadership. This helps them develop the ability to sense and sense-make, explore and evaluate, and shape and adapt to their preferred futures.

Figure 36
Qualities of the futures-ready organization,
with Anticipatory Leadership and
Participatory Organizational capabilities

This development and mastery naturally require intent, training, practice, patience, persistence and time.

THE CONCRETE LOOK AND FEEL OF
THE FUTURES-READY ORGANIZATION

During my conversations with progressive leaders and encounters with different organizations over the past decade, I have seen a distinct pattern among those who are futures-ready.

They want to stay modern.

They want to change and adapt to the developments around them.

They do not settle for being 'fast followers.'

They push power and mandate out to the teams.

They prefer small and nimble teams, carried forward by a strong and adaptable organizational platform.

They rethink and redesign decision-making mechanisms to tap into the collective intelligence and increase speed.

They operate in iterations of six-month intervals (April to September, October to March), deliberately out of sync with the fiscal year.

They are visionary, even in times of trouble.

They make horizon scanning a built-in habit in their rhythms.

They're playful, and experiment and engage in exploring new trends and possibilities.

They have organizational consciousness.

They intercept internal signals and movements early on, to explore and evaluate them.

They learn.

They mix and match the philosophies and methodologies of humanism, self-managed teams, flat organization, role-based work and purpose-driven collaboration.

They have a built-in drive for auto-adaptation — that is, the organization shape-shifts from the inside, according to its own needs, without a prompt or leadership team directive to trigger it.

They create the organizational infrastructure, in which numerous micro-enterprises can live.

They are ready for multiple, alternative futures.

In my experience, there's no single design that works for every organization. Even within a large company, different designs are needed depending on the part of the value chain, the national and demographic context, and the function. Additionally, the best design is local and temporary, as the ecosystem constantly changes.

There is no blueprint for the modern, futures-ready organization.

Instead, there is an invitation and a call to action to increase your Futures Literacy, apply Futures Thinking, evaluate the trends and signals, and design that organization that is feasible in the moment, in your context.

Use the Future to make decisions today about your structures, cultures and governance.

SHAPING YOUR OWN STRUCTURES, CULTURES AND GOVERNANCE

Let us revisit the original problem that we're looking at:

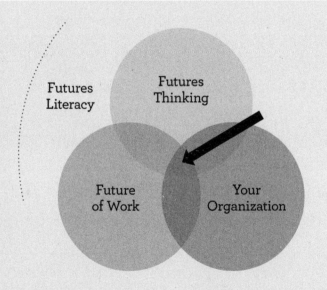

HOW DO I USE FUTURES THINKING
AS A VEHICLE TO CONTEXTUALIZE
THE FUTURE OF WORK ON THE INSIDE
OF MY ORGANIZATION?

Futures Literacy

Futures Thinking

Future of Work

Your Organization

We use the mechanisms from Futures Thinking to explore how the external and internal trends and signals affect you, and what scenarios emerge.

Then, what does that mean for the structures, the cultures and the governance in our organization?

In PART ONE of this book, we identified the common inhibitors to using Futures Thinking inside the organization:

- The challenge of scale of magnitude
- The challenges of 'I did not ask for options, I asked for a plan'

As listed in the beginning of this section, several characteristics are fundamentally different when using Futures Thinking on the inside of the organization, like the timeframe, organizational scope and the origin of the trends and signals. It is crucial for business owners, change champions, sponsors and business catalysts to acknowledge: (a) The existence of these trends and signals; (b) The effect they might have on the organization; (c) Their potential facilitation of alternative futures where the structures, cultures and governance are affected and need redesign.

Given a specific, detailed scenario and alternative future:

- What organizational **structures** does that scenario require?
- What does **governance** look like in that scenario?
- What are the **cultural** components in that scenario?

With that, what does the Backcasting exercise teach you regarding the establishment of these?
- What needs to be changed?
- What needs to be removed?
- What needs to be freshly created?

Please note that **we are investigating the alternative future before we look at the changes**. We do not create a baseline of the present, as this will anchor us and might lead to rudimentary extrapolation and uninformed planning. We reframe, and then we rethink.

We stand in the future, design from the future and strategize from the future.

THE MODELS FOR DISCUSSING AND ANALYSING THE DESIGN OF THE FUTURE ORGANIZATION

Here are the models that I constantly return to as lenses and discussion catalysts in these workshops, when we explore the design of the future organization prior to a transformation:

Models for exploring the paradoxical, opposite forces in an organization

1. The 5+5 Sliders of opposite forces in an organization
2. The guide to choosing your SALT-mix

Models for exploring governance and culture

3. The OS Canvas, conceived by transformation coach Aaron Dignan in *Brave New Work*[75]
4. The Culture Design Canvas, as coined by Gustavo Razzetti, Fearless Culture, www.fearlessculture.design[76]

Models for exploring the business model and value proposition for the external market and internal collaborators

5. The Business Model Canvas, by Strategyzer[77]
6. The Value Proposition Canvas, also from Strategyzer[78]

Models for exploring the structure that supports teams, collaboration and coordination efforts

7. The Alignment/Autonomy exercise from tech advisor Mark Richman[79]
8. The *From Command to Team-of-Teams* model, co-authored by Gen. Stanley McChrystal[80]
9. The 9-Grid model for the ecosystem around a team[81]

Items 3–8 are well-known, proven tools and canvases that are described elsewhere. I co-designed tools 1, 2 and 9, and they've been adjusted over the past decade, via action learning in hundreds of situations where organizational transformations have taken place. They will be introduced below, using the trends and signals from Trend Receivers that are quoted throughout the book.

The 5+5 Sliders

The Guide to choosing your SALT-mix

Culture Design Canvas, by Gustavo Razzetti, FearlessCulture, www.fearlessculture.design

Business Model Canvas. Copyright Strategyzer AG, strategyzer.com

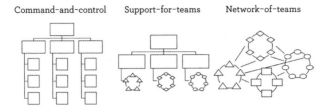

The 'From Command to
Team of Teams' model

The OS Canvas by Aaron
Dignan and The Ready

The Alignment/
Autonomy 2x2

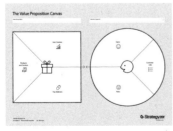

Value Proposition Canvas.
Copyright Strategyzer AG,
strategyzer.com

9-grid model for
the ecosystem

COMBINING SIGNALS WITH SCENARIOS TO DESIGN THE ORGANIZATION: APPLYING THE APPROACH TO THE SIGNALS IN THIS BOOK

Throughout these pages, you have found reports from so-called Trend Receivers from the US, Europe and Asia Pacific, sharing what they see and sense in and around diverse organizations. Although there are variations in what they encounter across geographies and business functions, there are clear commonalities:

Regarding people
Signal 1: Humanization of work. Focus on care, authenticity and meaningfulness.

Signal 2: A polarized view on Work from Home (WFH) and work flexibility.

Signal 3: Diversity, Equity and Inclusion (DEI) driven from the bottom of the organization.

Regarding technology, especially AI
Signal 4: Technological impact and concerns. Massive potential; overwhelming anxiety.

Regarding business
Signal 5: Pace and profit, accelerating speed, a preference toward momentum.

Signal 6: Shift from vision-based to reality-based management.

Regarding ecosystems thinking
Signal 7: Sustainability, ESG on the agenda across the value chain.

Let's assume, for the sake of the storytelling, that you've sorted these signals according to their likelihood of affecting you, and by the general likeability of the effect. It could end like this:

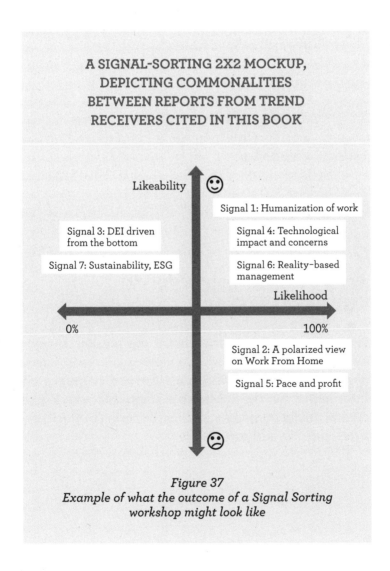

A SIGNAL-SORTING 2X2 MOCKUP, DEPICTING COMMONALITIES BETWEEN REPORTS FROM TREND RECEIVERS CITED IN THIS BOOK

Likeability ☺

Signal 1: Humanization of work

Signal 3: DEI driven from the bottom

Signal 4: Technological impact and concerns

Signal 7: Sustainability, ESG

Signal 6: Reality-based management

Likelihood

0%   100%

Signal 2: A polarized view on Work From Home

Signal 5: Pace and profit

☹

Figure 37
Example of what the outcome of a Signal Sorting workshop might look like

Let's then assume that we create a single scenario that represents our plausible and preferable future.

Scenario:
- A plausible and preferable future, with the signals that are likely to affect us (high likelihood), and where we like the effect (high likeability)
  › Signal 1: Humanization of work. Focus on care, authenticity and meaningfulness
  › Signal 4: Technological impact and concerns. Massive potential; overwhelming anxiety
  › Signal 6: Shift from vision-based to reality-based management
- In this scenario, we find Signal 2 and Signal 5 likely to happen, but we don't like the effect
- Similarly, we find Signal 3 and Signal 7 attractive, but do not consider them likely to affect us

START YOUR DESIGN FROM THE PARADOXES

First, we will analyse the balance and possible paradox within the underlying opposite forces and organizational dynamics in this scenario. **This exercise is immensely informative for the subsequent steps, and serves as a critical model for understanding the design of the structures, cultures and governance.**

THE 5+5 SLIDERS OF OPPOSITE FORCES

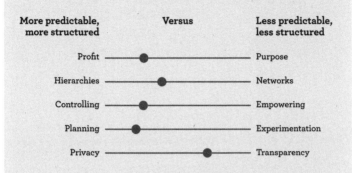

More predictable, more structured	Versus	Less predictable, less structured

Profit ——————— Purpose

Hierarchies ——————— Networks

Controlling ——————— Empowering

Planning ——————— Experimentation

Privacy ——————— Transparency

Figure 38
The 5 sliders inspired by the manifesto
from Responsive Org

This model is inspired by the manifesto from the Responsive Org community,[82] illustrating the characteristics of two types of organization: one built for prediction and the other for adaption. The model pulls the two sets of characteristics apart, installing a slider in between to enable nuances and contextual mixes of the specific opposite forces.

In the scenario above, the sliders are positioned to highlight the signal of a shift from vision-based to reality-based management, with a stronger focus on pace and profit, but still with the transparency that a more people-first, work-from-home organization needs.

Use the model to discuss how the opposite forces must be balanced in the scenario you're looking at.

There will be other tensions or opposite forces that you would want to investigate. Here are the five additional tensions I've found useful to discuss when designing alternative futures for the organization.

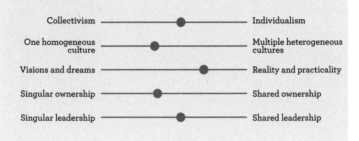

Figure 39
The 5 additional sliders, which are useful
for organizational design

With this in hand, you might want to be inspired by existing New Ways of Working paradigms, to describe the principles and methodologies that can support the future scenario we're working with. This is one of several times in this Using the Future approach where you have to consciously dismantle your bias and beliefs, and open up to seeing things anew.

Over the past decades, a small number of paradigms have emerged and proven to be robust, replicable and attractive.[83] Those are Sociocracy, Agile, Lean Start-up and Teal (SALT), which we've referenced here before. In short, they are characterized in the following ways:

- Sociocracy: A circular structure with roles, self-organizing teams, a purpose hierarchy and decision-making by consent[84]
- Agile: Adaptive planning, continual delivery and improvement, and rapid responses to change[85]

- Lean Start-up: Fast-paced 'build-measure-learn' cycles, autonomy as a team and the ability to pivot[86]
- Teal: Self-management, wholeness and evolutionary purpose as principles[87]

By far, the majority of those who embrace New Ways of Working establish their organizations as a mix of these SALT components. The RNAHub at Roche, which we profiled earlier, uses Teal as principles, Sociocracy as structure components, and the iterative approach from Agile and Scrum.

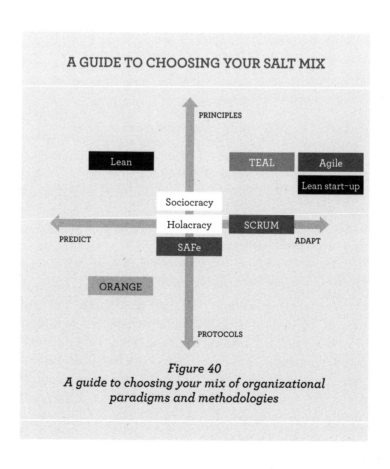

Figure 40
A guide to choosing your mix of organizational paradigms and methodologies

The SALT paradigms can be characterized by their principle-based versus protocol-based nature, and their focus on prediction versus adaption. They and their related paradigms can be depicted in a 2x2 like this. The model supports you as a guide to methodologies you could embrace or be inspired by, depending on your need for prediction/adaptation, and your organizational request for directive principles or descriptive protocols.

In this scenario, with the 5 Sliders mostly leaning to the left (predictive) side, you might have a logical preference for the so-called 'orange' culture, as described by Laloux as hierarchical, with management by objectives and optimization for productivity. However, it would be a modern version, as described by the academic Gary Hamel and management consultant Michele Zanini in *Humanocracy*, and with a huge splash of adaptation, as in the 'Participatory Organization' described earlier here.

Use the model to codify the characteristics of the organizational cultures that are needed or preferred, and use that as a starting point for your discussion. Remember to embrace the idea of the Participatory Organization, that enables adaptability by involving employees in the exploration and decision-making process.

This model was developed by Good Morning April in 2022 and has been further refined by me.

Next, the exploration of either governance and culture or business model and value proposition is almost always a muddled mix of back-and-forth, causality-and-correlation, and 'culture eats strategy for breakfast' discussions. It seems like these deliberations are inherently contextual and depend on the participants and the organizational Anticipatory Assumptions and myths they've uncovered during previous explorations.

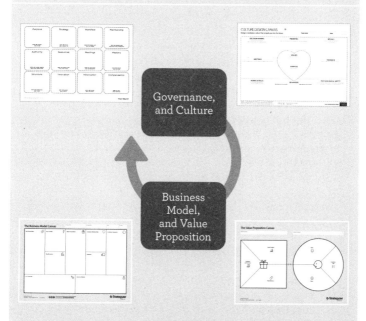

Figure 41
Four recommended models for exploring
the governance, culture and business model,
as a consequence of the Futures Thinking process

OS Canvas: Copyright by The Ready
Culture Design Canvas: Copyright by Gustavo Razzetti,
FearlessCulture, www.fearlessculture.design
Business Model Canvas: Copyright by Strategyzer AG,
strategyzer.com
Value Proposition Canvas: Copyright by Strategyzer AG,
strategyzer.com

The preferences for governance affect the culture, and vice versa.

The preferences for the business model and the value proposition affect the governance, and thus the culture.

In our scenario there is a need for a shift from vision-based to reality-based management, while still honouring the human side of the organization. To respond to the need for pace and profit, what is the business model going to look like? How do you then describe the supporting governance for that? And what culture would we prefer, to help ensure a workplace that is flexible and humane? Clearly, the four models above will affect each other in this scenario, creating valuable outcomes for the future of the organization.

Use these models in sync with each other, starting where you have the most obvious clarity. Or, you can be bold and start where you have the strongest uncertainty or friction, to learn from what irritates or bothers you.

Again, remember to embrace the idea of the Participatory Organization: What governance mechanisms must be in place for that? What cultural traits support it?

The final explorations relate to the structure of the organization, so that it supports the scenario and this alternative future that we're investigating.

We have three aspects to consider:
- Collaboration inside teams
- Coordination between teams
- The ecosystem under and around all teams

Your first questions to explore are related to how homogeneous the structure needs to be.

THE ALIGNMENT/AUTONOMY 2X2

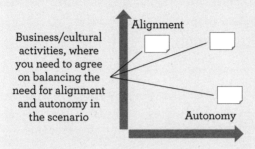

Business/cultural
activities, where
you need to agree
on balancing the
need for alignment
and autonomy in
the scenario

Figure 42
The Alignment/Autonomy 2x2 matrix

Does the future scenario foster a design where all teams work in the same way and where all the coordination mechanisms work in the same way? Or, does the scenario call for a heterogeneous structure with local variants and local dialects?

Related to the discussion of the 5 Sliders and the culture, how do you balance the need for alignment versus autonomy in the teams in this future? How can we have both at the same time, while properly supporting the teams?

In our scenario, it seems like there is a stronger need for alignment than for autonomy. Yet, there might be a need for a heterogeneous approach to encourage local cultures, to embrace the signal about the human workplace.

Use the model with specific cases from the scenario to pinpoint the preferred mix. Your detailed scenario description is immensely helpful here.

The big consultancies Deloitte[88] and McKinsey[89] have both in the last decade showcased how the classic hierarchy has been augmented with hybrid structures, ranging from traditional top-down structures to the team-of-team approach, as inspired by Gen. McChrystal.[90]

THE 'FROM COMMAND TO TEAM OF TEAMS' MODEL

Command-and-control   Support-for-teams   Network-of-teams

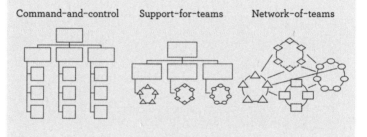

Figure 43
The 'From Command to Team of Teams' model,
adapted from Gen. McChrystal

Which of these will support the future scenario, considering the discussions above regarding governance and culture? Do you need a mix of these designs, with local dialects of culture and governance? Which approach fits with what part of the value chain?

In our scenario, a 'Command of Teams' or rather 'Support-for-Teams' approach seems applicable.

Use the detailed scenarios, along with the output from the Business Model Canvas, to investigate which design is fruitful in the business model.

Adding to this, evolutionary psychologist Robin Dunbar — known for his theory that people only have the bandwidth to maintain a finite number of interpersonal connections, 'Dunbar's 150' — and his team at the University of Liverpool have investigated the preferences for group sizes, such as in organizations and communities.[91] They conclude that "humans spontaneously form groups of preferred sizes organized in a geometrical series approximating 3–5, 9–15, 30–45, etc." This gives us guidelines for how we can imagine our organization. In my experience, these group sizes correspond perfectly to collaboration, coordination and identity:

- Teams of approximately 5 collaborate well
- Teams of approximately 15 coordinate well
- Teams of approximately 50 maintain a shared identity well

How do we also take this into account when discussing the structure, or structures, of our future organization?

One final model for discussing the structures, cultures and governance in the scenario is to look at the context for the teams. That is, consider the design of the ecosystem around the team. In my book from 2020, *Teal Dots in an Orange World*, I codified this 9-Grid model as a lens through which to view the cultural, decision-making and coordination mechanisms around a team or a business unit.

THE 9-GRID MODEL FOR THE ECOSYSTEM AROUND A TEAM

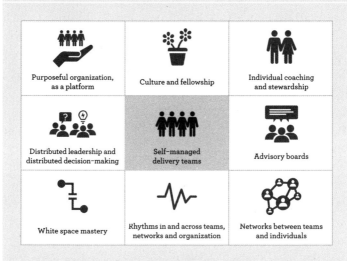

Figure 44
The 9-Grid model for the ecosystem around a team

Top row: What culture is needed for the team to be sufficiently self-led in this scenario?
Middle row: What clarifications are needed for the decision-making mechanisms in this scenario?
Bottom row: What discussions are needed for coordination with the other teams, business units and stakeholders in this scenario?

In our scenario, it seems that the decision-making mechanisms are in particular need of attention.

Use the model to discuss which of the elements around the team and the business unit stay the same, and which of them need a redesign as part of the transformation – and to enable the Participatory Organization.

With the nine models above you can discuss, evaluate and explore the structures, cultures and governance that fit with the scenario you're imagining. This can be used for storytelling, engagement and creating emotional responses that flow into the understanding of your transformation effort and initiatives.

Logical next steps from this are:

- Backcasting, to understand the activities and elements that need to be in place
- Planning and roadmapping
- Careful execution of the transformation, with frequent revisiting of the trends and signals, scenarios, Anticipatory Assumptions and myths, and Future-casting/Backcasting/Forecasting activities

What I'm hinting at here is that 'Using the Future' is not a one-off activity, just as change and transformation are ongoing pursuits that must take into consideration the dynamic ecosystem around you. This is also why Strategic Foresight activities are a continuous focus for organizations, as the global ecosystem is in constant flux.

Listen to the signals. Consider the trends.

Explore the scenarios in due time.

Plan for change and transformation, but plan from the future.

Rinse, repeat.

REFLECTIONS FROM PART THREE

In this section we have applied the tools and mechanisms from Futures Thinking inside our organization.

We discussed what changes when we flip the approach from the outside, where it's born and developed, to the inside: aim, scope, time horizon, origin of signals and ownership.

We combined the tools into a coherent approach: The Double L Double A Double E method.

We discussed three areas that deserve special attention when applying Futures Thinking inside the organization: (1) Internal signals; (2) Assumptions and myths; (3) Shaping the structures, cultures and governance, as they would fit in the scenario.

In general, we underlined that designing your transformation, and your organization, should happen 'from the future.'

We use the future to make decisions today. We design the organization from the future.

We have now answered three of the four questions that we set out to:

- How do I use my understanding of trends and signals in society and technology to design my organization, culture and governance?
- How do I look for signals inside my organization?
- How do I challenge and revisit our assumptions and myths, upon which we build our view of the future?

What is missing is the last question:

- **What kind of anticipatory leadership does it take to be futures literate inside my organization?**

SUMMARY

This chapter focused on applying the mechanisms from Futures Thinking on the inside of the organization, when we set sail for the transformation.

Double L is the mechanism of Signal Sorting according to Likelihood and Likeability.

Double A is the approach to uncovering Anticipatory Assumptions.

Double E is the way to Explore and Evaluate scenarios and alternative futures.

Internal signals are of special interest to us.

Organizational assumptions and myths will surface during the workshops and action-learning.

And this enables us to discuss **the Participatory Organization** and the structures, culture and governance that are part of the organizational architecture for this alternative future.

In turn, this supports us in imagining the transformation and storytelling about the activities and about where we're going.

We are activating and training for our tactical foresight.

This prepares us for PART FOUR, discussing Anticipatory Leadership, the requisite skills and capacities, the emotional response to Using the Future, tackling VUCA and BANI, and agency.

TRENDS AND SIGNALS, SENSED AND RECEIVED BY TRAVIS MARSH
Coach and Co-Founder, Human First Works
Co-Author of *Lead Together: The Bold, Brave, Intentional Path to Scaling Your Business.*

Location: USA

- Knowledge management and AI:
  AI is supercharging knowledge management within organizations, leading to a shift in how information is processed and utilized. This has implications for how quickly new employees can become impactful and the importance of discernment in handling information.

- Polarities in organizational dynamics:
  An increase of divergent views within organizations, such as openness vs. transparency, self-managed teams vs. hierarchies. Often one side in such differences is hidden or overlooked.

- Explosion of goals and measurements:
  There's an increase in the quantity of goals and measurements, leading to a decrease in their meaningfulness and a lack of discipline in focusing on what truly matters.

- Increased connections and networks:
  Especially at junior levels, there's a noticeable increase in external interfacing and networking, affecting trust and transparency within organizations.

- Rapid change and Lean Startup-mentality:
  An agile, Lean Startup approach is becoming
  essential in all sectors, not just startups.

- Adult development and mindfulness:
  There's a growing focus on personal and
  professional development, including
  mindfulness and emotional intelligence.

- Shift from individual to team excellence:
  The focus is shifting from individual
  achievements to team-based performance,
  though there's a lack of understanding about
  effective team formation.

- Trauma-organizations:
  More organizations are becoming aware
  of and sensitive to the traumas and
  psychological safety of their employees.

- Proliferation of coaching and its challenges:
  Coaching is recognized as vital at all
  organizational levels, but there's a gap in
  effective leadership coaching skills.

- Job hopping vs. long-term commitment:
  There's a trend of frequent job changes
  among some, while others are finding
  deeper connections and purposes within
  their roles.

- Fractionalization of organizations:
  More modular, less hierarchically
  structured organizations are appearing.

CASE STUDY: JUST IMAGINE BEING 1,000 EMPLOYEES IN A FLAT HIERARCHY

Who

Pingala A/S is a Danish IT consultancy in the enterprise resource planning (ERP), customer relationship management (CRM) and business intelligence (BI) domains, delivering Microsoft D365FO, CRM and BI advice and solutions.

Founded in 2008, Pingala has grown from a two-person operation into a company with more than 130 employees in three locations in Denmark and offices in Oslo and Dubai.

Elements from 'Using the Future'
- Futures Readiness
- Signal Sorting
- Internal Signals
- Futurecasting, repeatedly
- Imagination and storytelling
- Backcasting and Forecasting
- Anticipatory Assumptions and myths

Approach

Pingala is a modern organization, inspired by Teal principles and Sociocratic practices, with a flat structure and no managers apart from the CEO, Kent Højlund.

The company is featured as a case study in my two previous books on the Future of Work, *The Responsive Leader* and *Teal Dots in an Orange World*.

When Højlund became CEO in 2013, he asked himself:

How can we successfully scale from 10 to 100 employees, AND stay true to the original idea of a company we would want to work in for the rest of our professional careers, with a flat organization and no managers?

In what ways do we need to differentiate ourselves relative to our ecosystem, partners, delivery mechanisms and culture, to attract the right talent and beat the competition?

Shortly after his arrival at Pingala, Højlund made two critical strategic principles clear:

First, working with culture as the primary strategic theme would catalyse execution of several vital strategic drives. This turned out to be a pattern he would repeat year after year in the coming decade.

Second, merely extrapolating from the past in the development of culture, structure, governance and approach to recruitment would not bring Pingala to the place they envisioned. Instead of working from the present, Højlund began strategizing from the future.

In 2015, the first Futurecasting/Backcasting/Forecasting workshops took place, to answer the question of how you grow from 10 to 100 employees in a flat organization with no managers.

"Maybe 50 people is the right amount," Højlund stated at the time. "But we need to imagine something larger to enable ourselves to rethink and redesign the mechanisms and the cultural glue."

The drive for growth came from several perspectives. First, as employees increasingly asked to be part of larger, more complex, international client projects, more people were needed. Second, customers were increasingly looking for end-to-end implementations, meaning that Pingala needed an even bigger team, with broader professional and cognitive diversity. And finally, there might soon be a talent pool drought in Denmark, leading Pingala and Højlund to cast their sights abroad and imagine locations elsewhere in Europe.

A few scenarios were established that looked out to something like a decade into the future, in which Pingala's workforce had grown to more than 100. During this process, internal signals and movements surfaced and were discussed to account for cultural movements. One mental image that Højlund used was that of traditional Viking ships. These were small, manoeuvrable, with a short chain of command, and all sailors had the skills to man any position.

Imagining the cultures, conversations, customer projects, Town Hall meetings, recruitment processes, locations and the decision-making in these alternative futures helped him pinpoint the elements that now needed to be redesigned or invented from scratch. Numerous elements and mechanisms would change, in a 100-employee company with no middle managers.

Several activities were initiated:
- Replacing the classic management-driven employee coaching with a peer-to-peer mentoring approach, called the Colleague Network Development Conversation
- The first training and workshops with Sociocracy and Holacracy were established
- Discussions were initiated about decision-making mechanisms in large, non-hierarchical groups,

taking the first stabs at answering the question 'Who decides *who decides?*' in a 100-person community
- The establishment of an annual Organizational Network Analysis to monitor the development in relationships and belonging

In 2019, as Pingala reached 50 employees, Højlund stepped up the pace, asking how the company could grow to 1,000 people while maintaining a flat organization, without managers.

"It is never about the number ONE THOUSAND," he said. "But if we solve for that, we might invent some solutions that help us today." This is a wonderful example of Using the Future to make decisions about today.

A process similar to Futurecasting was embraced, imagining and storytelling about daily life in a flat, managerless, thousand-employee operation. How would communication flow? How would customer projects be established, orchestrated and assigned? How about internal training, and taking care of each other? What about local cultural dialects? And locations? How many would there be, and where? How would you have a Town Hall meeting with such a far-flung workforce?

This Futurecasting for alternative scenarios for Pingala was followed by a Backcasting and Forecasting exercise, just as before. Among the focus items were:
- Strengthening the work with Circles, Roles and delegation of mandate
- Adjusting the peer-to-peer mentoring mechanism
- Adjusting the onboarding and buddy system
- Launching a podcast, featuring interviews with employees

Each of these elements are catalysts for a decentralized culture and leadership approach that mitigated the need for a central bottleneck. As Højlund said back then, "I want to lead the organization, but not lead the employees. I don't want to steer. I want to create the ability for the employees to steer, when needed. Often it is a matter of removing myself from the equation and letting the employees drive the work and the decisions. That will scale!"

Three years later, in 2022, as Pingala crossed the mythical 100-employee mark, roughly half of the company was invited to a 'Use the Future' community-driven event. The first exercise was to poll and map out the employees' futures-readiness. Among the questions they were asked: How much do you think the world and Pingala are going to change in the next ten years? And, how much influence do you feel you have on the futures of the company?

The next task was to jointly imagine Pingala in the year 2032, ten years on. And then, divided into six teams for a two-hour Signal Sorting exercise around trends and signals for the Future of Work, the Future of Technology and global megatrends, they were asked to imagine and describe three different, alternative Pingalas. Helpfully, one group went on to create a pessimistic, negative scenario, as a counterweight to the optimism in the room.

After presenting and storytelling about them, one scenario was selected as the 'Pingala 2032' which they then backcasted from. A big wall was filled with drawings, Post-its and artefacts from this plausible and preferable future, making the scenario very visible to the employees as they stood in front of it all, actively discussing it.

Then, everybody took three steps backwards, pretending they were now two years before that Pingala. Everything was reconsidered from that point in time and notes were taken on what actions needed to be in place in 2030 for the 2032 future to become real. Again, three steps backwards, and they were now in the year 2028. Eventualities were discussed and notes were taken. This was repeated a few times, and within the hour a full backcast roadmap for 2024, 2026, 2028 and 2030 had taken shape.

The roadmap consisted of four tracks: (a) Culture; (b) Size and structure; (c) Technology and solutions; (d) Customers.

Now, in 2024, Pingala has in fact reached 130 employees and is steadily growing.

___

Outcome and impact
Clearly, imagining the futures for Pingala supported both the establishment of the scalable solutions and the discussions of risks and risk-taking. Vital dialogues emerged around what drives growth, what success looks like, who has which viewpoints, and what might break the cultural bonds, highlighting the assumptions and myths in the organization.

Not everyone found the activities completely engaging or easy to grasp, but there was a general buzz of engagement, ownership and agency in the room.

INTERLUDE: FUN WAYS TO GET FAMILIAR WITH SIGNALS

This first appeared in 'Futures of Work: Horizon Scanning Document 2023,' published that year by Good Morning April, and has been adapted for the context here. [92]

"Futures thinking is just voodoo and hocus-pocus."

"I could do that too. It's just like fortune telling by looking at coffee grounds or tea leaves."

"So, tell me (giggles), can you predict the future?"

Maybe you've heard similar reactions, or had them yourself. Admittedly, years ago I was sceptical. However, diving into the science and the practical application of Futures Thinking has opened my mind, broadened my perspective and altered my stance.

Futures Thinking has nothing to do with fortune telling or supernatural forces. It is very much rooted in the present, embracing and understanding our approach to assumptions and anticipation, flexing our imagination, and facilitating conversation about preferences for possible futures.

Let's look at three concrete ways to use some of the many mechanisms and tools from Futures Thinking in your daily work.

Maybe, as I was, you'll get inspired.

1: CREATING YOUR OWN 'HUH, THAT'S ODD' DATABASE AT WORK

I bet you already do this with friends, with your team members, or over dinner with your family: You share odd things you've found online.

"I found this pair of glasses that Google makes. It listens to our conversation, translates it in real time, and shows the result on the inside of the lenses. In that way, I can have subtitles on the conversation with Mårten when he speaks Swedish." Your reaction might be, "So cool," or "How utterly useless." Or, maybe, "Wow, scary — talk about surveillance!"

Whatever your reaction, you have just found a signal: A concrete example of something that might grow and snow-ball into a trend. This is what we futurists do when we scan the news, scroll through our digital feeds, and look at soci-etal behaviour. We look for anomalies, for things that make us go, "Huh, that's odd."

Here's something you can try: Make it a habit that each of you in your team brings a signal you've picked up on to your next monthly meeting. Share them with each other and make note of your emotional responses. Over time, you end up with a signal database within your professional domain, be it on the future of food, the future of TV, or whatever is relevant to your sector and areas of interest.

Also, in this way you build a habit of scanning for signals everywhere, all the time. It has absolutely become a habit of mine. Some of us dedicate 5–8 hours a week to scanning for signals, consciously or subconsciously.

2: PLAYING 'IF THIS, THEN THAT ... AND THAT, AND THAT'

Another game that futurists play is to let a signal unfold, and unfold, and unfold.

You have maybe tried the "Yes, and ..." improv method when brainstorming a solution, or as an icebreaker at a business event. This is the same thing: Build upon the existing idea with yet another idea. This time, however, the seed for the conversation is the signal.

Let's consider the Google Glasses again. Here's how the commentary might freely flow:

"If that becomes reality, then people in multicultural suburbs will be able to understand each other. People who speak Danish would understand the Arabs, who could understand the Germans, who'd understand the Swedes. This might lead to more relationships being built, friendships, and a more peaceful world. Maybe we can get subtitles to what our cats and dogs try to say to us. And people who are deaf can listen in on all conversations and become a stronger part of society. Maybe my old grandma with Alzheimer's can get hints on who she's with, so she doesn't feel so isolated. Maybe the glasses can interpret facial expressions and help people with autism who have difficulty doing that. And maybe the glasses can read lips too. Oh, but then people could eavesdrop on my whispered conversations with business partners and steal our ideas. Or use them for surveilling me and violating my privacy."

This technique strengthens your imagination and is a well-known way to poke around with possible consequences — that is, with possible futures. Futurist and researcher Jerome C. Glenn spun it into a game called 'The Futures Wheel.'

3: PLAYING 'THIS IS GOOD NEWS FOR ...'
There's a big difference between these possible futures and the preferable futures.

Not all the possible futures are likable for YOU. People will prefer a certain flavour or variant of those possibilities, and their preference is not necessarily going to be YOURS. Their future may not be one that YOU would like to see unfold. A classic mechanism for evaluating signals is to sort them in a 2x2 matrix according to likelihood of impact and likeability of the effect. This is the Signal Sorting we discussed earlier.

However, this game is different: We strive to investigate WHO each of these possible futures is good for, even those futures that we dislike ourselves.

"Google Glasses used for surveillance can be good for undercover cops."

"People with hearing disabilities, who have a hard time navigating in group situations, can regain their ability to keep track of a conversation."

"People who work in noisy surroundings, like firemen, might be able to communicate in a different way."

Again, this is a method that can help strengthen your imagination.

Futurist and strategic forecaster Joseph Voros devised the so-called Futures Cone to unpack the different potential futures: The preposterous, the possible, the plausible, the projected, the probable, and finally, the preferable future.

The approach here, for each of the possible futures, is to imagine WHO this might be good for. Who is it out there who would prefer THAT version of the future?

TRY IT — GIVE IT A SPIN
These are fun and entertaining games that can also be useful for training employees in your Futures Thinking, making that exercise a habit, and applying it in your work.

Oh, and by the way, fortune telling through tea leaves or coffee grounds is called tasseography.

PART FOUR:

THE ANTICIPATORY LEADERSHIP — MINDSET, CAPABILITIES, IMPACT AND AGENCY

In this part we want to answer the last of the four questions we set out to investigate:

- What kind of anticipatory leadership does it take to be futures literate inside my organization?

We'll look at the professional literature and resources highlighting the capabilities of futurists who've mastered Strategic Foresight. And then, we'll augment it with observations from action-learning by the leaders who master Tactical Foresight inside the organization.

Finally, we will focus on the impact of Using the Future and increasing Futures Literacy in organizations. This will leverage sensing, agency and mitigating feelings of VUCA and BANI that we addressed in PART ONE.

THE NEED FOR ANTICIPATORY LEADERSHIP

Let us start with a refresher on the problem we're trying to solve, which we unpacked here earlier. The hundreds of conversations I've had with progressive leaders revealed three patterns:

One, they need to transform their organization in order to adapt to the changing ecosystem around them, in society and technology, externally and internally. At the same time, there is a need for increased change-readiness.

Two, there is a lack of certainty about how to move ahead. The familiar, by-the-book answers are increasingly insufficient, or they need a twist to fit the context or solve the problem.

And three, more and more of these leaders were using phrases like 'I think,' 'I feel' and 'I sense,' hinting at an emerging style that: (a) Is not solely based on transactional behaviour;

(b) Is oriented toward seemingly emotional and intuition-based capabilities.

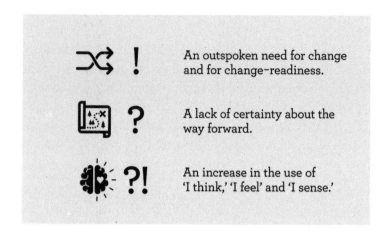

⤨	**!**	An outspoken need for change and for change-readiness.
🗺	**?**	A lack of certainty about the way forward.
🧠	**?!**	An increase in the use of 'I think,' 'I feel' and 'I sense.'

This sort of sentiment is representative of the dialogue: "I read all the trend reports from McKinsey, Microsoft, Copenhagen Institute for Futures Studies, and so on. I really want to take that into consideration when I design our transformation, but my role is inside the organization, not in a strategic, outward-facing function. What can I do?"

Another typical reaction would be: "I'm in favour of Teal as a principle and co-leadership as a practice, but are these the right ways forward at this time? The current people and HR trends are contradictory to the trends in business and the global economy. How do I move forward? How do I use these insights to design my transformation?"

The approach that we investigate in this book is to get inspired by Futures Literacy, Futures Thinking and Strategic Foresight, and flip all the methodologies to the inside of the organization. Two questions arise once that is done:

From the outside-in, what changes by using the Futures Thinking methodologies on the inside of the organization?

From the inside-out, how can we take trends and signals into account when we investigate and describe the possible scenarios for our transformations inside our organization?

We sought to answer those questions in PART TWO and PART THREE. However, the remaining challenges are captured in these sorts of questions:

What sort of leadership does it take?

What mindset is required?

What are the attributes and capabilities of a leader who masters this?

What positive impact can be achieved in the process?

The Anticipatory Leadership that is needed for embracing and applying Futures Thinking is different from traditional transactional and executional leadership, in several ways. You need to master Futures Literacy and be able to reveal, reframe and rethink your own — and your colleagues' — assumptions and myths. You need to be able to imagine how trends and signals unfold, and express your personal level of desirability of those signals. You should be able to spot the internal signals and engage with the internal Trend Receivers. Standing in the Future and Future-casting requires imagination and storytelling. Finally, you need to express the consequences of the scenarios, in terms of changes to the structures, cultures and governance needed in these alternative futures. Clearly, that calls for fresh, new skills that go beyond those common to traditional leadership.

Let's take a closer look at that.

EXISTING SOURCES THAT DESCRIBE QUALITIES OF FUTURE-ORIENTED LEADERSHIP

Various sources have described qualities and capabilities of leadership for Strategic Foresight or what it takes to be a futurist leader.

In "The Anticipatory Leader: Futurist, Strategist and Integrator,"[93] management consultants Michael Sales and Anika Savage describe three key traits of anticipatory leaders:

- Futurist
- Strategist
- Integrator

In "Meet the Future-Minded Leader: Your Organization's Answer to Uncertainty,"[94] entrepreneur Adam Wood lists three skills of future-minded leaders:

- Optimism
- Pragmatism
- Envisioning potential outcome

In "Five Principles for Thinking Like a Futurist,"[95] researcher and consultant Marina Gorbis lists these principles for behaviour:

- Forget about predictions
- Focus on signals
- Look back to see forward
- Uncover patterns
- Create a community

These are just a few examples, and an abundance of resources exist highlighting the role, skills, capabilities, mindset or behaviour of a futurist leader. However, the vast majority of the material focuses on some variant of

Strategic Foresight for market purposes, not on the characteristics of a leader who applies Futures Thinking to the inside of the organization. One of the sources that actually does provide an organizational perspective is "Exploring the Lived Experience of Individual Foresight in Organizations."[96] Here, the academic Melissa Innes describes Individual Foresight characteristics as seen from the perspective of HR professionals. These include:

- Past experience
- Future thinking (visualization)
- Mental time travel (imagining/remembering)
- Temporal preference
- Openness to experience
- Episodic foresight

She also highlights the need for intuition.

There seem to be some similarities between mindsets and one's skills, and especially the need for imagination and the ability to rethink the existing. What I am curious about is **uncovering the mindset, skills, capabilities and behaviour of anticipatory, future-oriented leaders** who use Futures Thinking for transformation and change management within their organizational ecosystem.

CAPABILITIES OF THE ANTICIPATORY LEADERSHIP

There is a very clear pattern that I've found via hundreds of dialogues with leaders, numerous Futures Thinking workshops and dozens of Using the Future journeys through the years. These participatory, action-learning methodologies have both uncovered and been used in training on these leadership traits.

In the overview below, I do not distinguish between traits, talents, capabilities, etc., as such characterization has turned out to be of less significant value to the leaders.

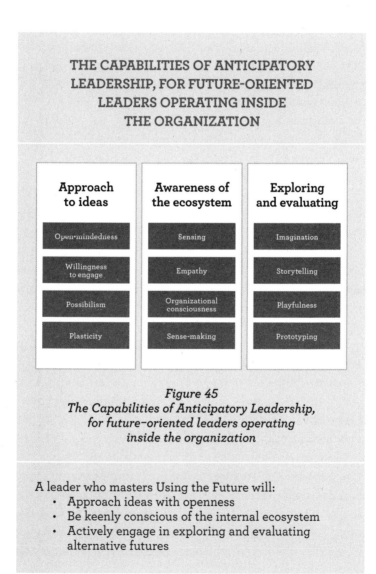

THE CAPABILITIES OF ANTICIPATORY LEADERSHIP, FOR FUTURE-ORIENTED LEADERS OPERATING INSIDE THE ORGANIZATION

Approach to ideas	Awareness of the ecosystem	Exploring and evaluating
Open-mindedness	Sensing	Imagination
Willingness to engage	Empathy	Storytelling
Possibilism	Organizational consciousness	Playfulness
Plasticity	Sense-making	Prototyping

Figure 45
The Capabilities of Anticipatory Leadership,
for future-oriented leaders operating
inside the organization

A leader who masters Using the Future will:
- Approach ideas with openness
- Be keenly conscious of the internal ecosystem
- Actively engage in exploring and evaluating alternative futures

Approach to ideas:

- **Open-mindedness** toward new, strange, unexpected ideas (and trends and signals) from diverse sources, without bias and prejudice
- **Willingness to engage** in exploring ideas and signals via conversations, dialogue, mind games and workshops
- **Possibilism**, the belief that the futures are not determined by context and ecosystem, but by human agency
- **Plasticity**, the ability to let go of previous beliefs in favour of new ideas, allowing for adaptation. 'Strong opinions, loosely held' is a mantra for the leader

Awareness of the ecosystem:

- **Sensing** is the ability to receive information from the surrounding ecosystem, and engage with intuition as a medium to pick up on unconventional signs and signals
- **Empathy** allows one to engage with others, relate to them and their situation, and perceive their point of view
- **Organizational consciousness** is tapping into the collective awareness, value system and shared cultural understanding of the group and ecosystem, and foreseeing emerging behavioural and cultural movements
- **Sense-making** is to give meaning to experiences, interpret the input and see patterns that may have only vague contours

Exploring and evaluating:
- **Imagination** is the ability to shape ideas, concepts and situations in the mind, vividly and engagingly
- **Storytelling** engages colleagues, creates emotional responses, shares experiences and connects people to people, as well as people to scenarios and alternative futures
- **Playfulness** is a fun, lighthearted, non-binding approach to shaping ideas, creating scenarios and solving problems
- **Prototyping** is needed for creating a real-life, early model that's used for exploring and evaluating the alternative future. It is taking one or two steps into realizing the idea and the scenario, and 'picking up a shovel' to start building

When we compare this list with the previously mentioned traits and capabilities of futures-ready leadership, as found in the professional literature, we find four distinct elements that differentiate future-oriented anticipatory leadership on the inside from that on the outside (the one engaged in Strategic Foresight). **These are possibilism, plasticity, playfulness and organizational consciousness.**

LEADERS WHO SUCCESSFULLY APPLY FUTURES THINKING INSIDE THEIR ORGANIZATION MASTER THESE TRAITS

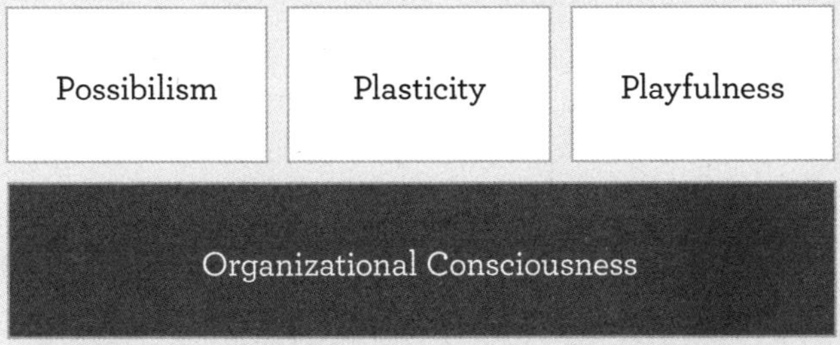

| Possibilism | Plasticity | Playfulness |

Organizational Consciousness

Figure 46
The four traits that Futures Thinking leaders master

Possibilism: They believe in human agency, not determinism
Plasticity: They believe in adaptation, not rigidity
Playfulness: They approach challenges with joy, creativity and spontaneity
Organizational Consciousness: They are aware of both the existing and emerging cultures in the ecosystem, including subcultural, hidden and rebellious movements

On possibilism: The leaders who master this trait believe in agency within their organizational ecosystem. They're confident they can change the future for the organization, and that the ecosystem and organizational context does not determine the solution, roadmap, structure, culture and governance. They genuinely believe that the existing ways of working can be altered, and that a disruption in the ecosystem is both possible and necessary.

Some of these leaders are visionaries, and can imagine and tell stories about the alternative futures they long for, engaging people and inviting them to help co-create the scenarios. Some are myth-busters, going up against organizational habits and assumptions, breaking rules and acting as rebels, often proving that they are right. The majority of the leaders exhibiting this trait of possibilism also have substantial business acumen, with enough organizational experiences with transformations under their belt to support and liberate them in their acts of agency.

On plasticity: The leaders who master plasticity have strong beliefs, opinions and perspectives, but they're also able to change their minds. They allow for adaptation and can let go of previous beliefs in favour of new visions, ideas, approaches or solutions. They have grit and believe in the Growth Mindset. They never see such changes as failure, but frame them as learning and collecting insights. "We had a learning moment," as Garry Ridge, former CEO of the lubricant manufacturer WD-40, expresses it. 'Strong opinions, loosely held' is a motto Jane McGonigal teaches her students in the Coursera curriculum on Futures Thinking. She positions it as a way to frame and express the trait of going all in, and having a strong opinion and personal perspective on the trend, signal, scenario or future you're looking at ... but being flexible and able to let it go in favour of other perspectives. Along the way, these leaders are also willing to handle the consequences of listening to the signals and exploring alternative futures. You might experience scenarios that are surprising, challenging, disruptive and uncomfortable. Deal with it.

On playfulness: The playful leaders augment the classic analytic-logic approach to problem solving with creativity, simulation games, 'Yes, and ...' prompts, curiosity and non-binding ideation activities. You might find these leaders with a stack of Post-its, a pile of LEGO bricks, or in front of a whiteboard, sketching, experimenting and imagining (im)possible solutions and scenarios. They also strive to create a culture of comfort for colleagues they invite into this world of playfulness. Some of them have studied the behavioural social science behind this approach and its exercises, and can explain to sceptics what's going on and why it can deliver meaningful results. But the majority of them engage with intuition, carried forward by their beliefs and many years of experience.

On Organizational Consciousness: The capability to zoom out and see patterns is second nature for the person who masters Anticipatory Leadership. They understand the real culture and have an intuition for spotting both opportunities and risks when planning for change and transformations. They're also able to sense subcultural, hidden, rebellious movements before they break through to the surface. These leaders are likeable and approachable, and people naturally open up and share insights and perspectives with them. Leaders who master this organizational consciousness are also adept at spotting internal signals, myths and assumptions, either firsthand or via the internal Trend Receivers they're in contact with. And, they have a deeply-rooted, albeit sometimes unconscious, ability to sense what is right and what is wrong. They are a wonderful and trustworthy ethical compass for the organization and its subcultures.

Here are a few reflective statements to help assess your Anticipatory Leadership skills. For each, indicate your level of agreement on a scale from 1 (Strongly Disagree) to 5 (Strongly Agree).

Possibilism

I actively explore and evaluate multiple alternative futures before making decisions.	1
	2
	3
	4
	5

I believe in agency and my ability to shape the future by exploring various possible alternatives.	1
	2
	3
	4
	5

When faced with uncertainty, I focus on creating opportunities rather than on the limitations.	1
	2
	3
	4
	5

Plasticity

I adapt my leadership style and strategies based on changing circumstances and new information.	1
	2
	3
	4
	5

I can let go of previous beliefs, plans and solutions in favour of new ideas, per the motto 'Strong opinions, loosely held.'	1
	2
	3
	4
	5

I view challenges and organizational friction as opportunities to understand, learn and grow, rather than as obstacles.	1
	2
	3
	4
	5

Playfulness

I incorporate elements of creativity, novelty and play in problem-solving and decision-making.	1 2 3 4 5
I nurture a culture where team members feel comfortable experimenting with new ideas.	1 2 3 4 5
I use playful exploration and spontaneity to create a culture of continuous learning.	1 2 3 4 5

Organizational Consciousness

I embrace the collective awareness, value systems and shared culture of our ecosystem.	1 2 3 4 5
I strive to understand and appreciate the diverse subcultures within our organization.	1 2 3 4 5
I can sense and foresee emerging behavioural and cultural movements, including the subcultural, hidden or rebellious ones.	1 2 3 4 5

DEVELOPING YOUR ANTICIPATORY LEADERSHIP CAPABILITIES

Futures Literacy, Futures Thinking and Anticipatory Leadership capabilities can be trained and developed.

> **Futures Literacy is the ability and capacity**
> to think critically and abstractly about the future.
> Key building blocks are the understanding
> of anticipation and assumptions.
>
> **Futures Thinking is the creative and investigative process** of exploring and evaluating what affects us,
> to describe scenarios for the futures.

As mentioned earlier, the experiences from one of these fields spill over to the other, act as resonance chambers and support your mastery there.

Educate yourself. Read. Listen. Watch. Check the list of recommendations at the back of this book.

Take courses to learn from experts and meet like-minded futurists. I recommend coursework offered by Copenhagen Institute for Futures Studies and the online Futures Thinking Specialization course on Coursera, created by Institute for the Future and Jane McGonigal.

Pay attention to trends and signals in the news, social media, newsletters, online forums and other outlets. Every time you stumble upon a signal, a prediction, an anomaly or a list of '10 trends to focus on,' ask yourself: (1) What is the bias of the author? (2) What is the likelihood of this trend affecting me, in my organization? (3) What is the likeability of the effect it will have, in my organization? (4) If this trend is not desirable for me, who would it appeal to?

Practice action-learning by applying the Using the Future methodology presented in PART TWO and PART THREE of this book.

Team up with others. Surround yourself with other Futurists. Futures Thinking is a team sport, as you will benefit immensely from other people's points of view, opinions and expressions of what's desirable to them.

When you initiate your Futures Thinking journey in your team, make sure that **you get the theory and terminology** clear from the start. "Theory is key," as the academic Jan Oliver Schwarz says, ranking it as the leading factor in the list of principles for working with Strategic Foresight.[97]

SENSING

You may have noticed it already.

Throughout my real-life observations of the challenges leaders face, and the world of Futures Literacy and Futures Thinking, there runs a striking red thread of something hard to grasp and seldomly discussed in business settings: Sensing.

Sensing the seemingly omnipresent, flowing just beneath the surface. Sensing the dynamics in the organization. Sensing the trends and signals in your business domain. Sensing what's emerging, nagging, happening and not happening. Sensing the unspoken.

Sensing and sense-making are two of the key capabilities associated with Anticipatory Leadership. As referenced earlier here, among the hundreds of leaders I've spoken to over the past few years regarding the shocks, shifts and changes in their organization and business domain, there is a clear increase in the use of phrases like 'I think,' 'I feel' and 'I sense.'

 An increase in the use of 'I think,' 'I feel' and 'I sense.'

These leaders — who are growing competent in Anticipatory Leadership — have engaged and discovered their ability to pick up and intercept signals from their organizations, their communities and from within themselves.

These experiences make them stop, think and change their approach — and change their conditions for change.

To clarify the definitions and terminology we're dealing with here:

Sensing refers to the automatic reception of sensory experiences, like sound, sight and emotions, without immediately interpreting or analysing them. **Sensing is about receiving information and input, as a medium.** We can add spirituality and soulfulness to this list, as sensing not only relates to the information from our five senses, but also takes into account the realms of nature, life and the universe. The term 'Deep Listening' is used to describe this approach.

Sense-making refers to the process of understanding and finding meaning in those sensory perceptions, informed by historical information and experiences you have amassed. Sense-making is about making sense of what you have sensed.

Deep Listening can be described as an ongoing practice of suspending self-oriented, reactive thinking and opening one's awareness to the unknown and unexpected.[98] Elements of this include active listening, mindfulness, meditation, regenerative practices and self-awareness.

IS SENSING A SKILL, A TALENT, A CAPABILITY?

You might say that sensing is an **innate talent** that we are born with. Most of us have our five traditional senses (sight, hearing, taste, smell and touch), and we possess others, like sensing temperature, pain, balance and so on.

You might say that sensing is a **skill** that you can train for, hone and master, like the sense one develops for the taste and smell of a specific type of food. Or a sense for jazz improvisation. It is learned and practised to perfection.

You might say that it is about **intuition**, empathy, connectivity with nature and near-spiritual emotions, and as such more abstract than the above examples.

My inspiration and teacher in this area, Alex Lambie, an artist and UNESCO Futures Literacy Fellow of Storytelling, describes it like this:

> "Sensing is life itself. I sense therefore we are.
>
> From that perspective, sensing is the medium in which we discover our talents and develop our skills.
>
> Being open to the true capacity of our senses (especially in the urgency of much of the 'modern world'), that perhaps is a skill, in so much as we need to practise being open and learn how to respond to what we receive, with discernment."
>
> — Alex Lambie, Artist and UNESCO Futures Literacy Fellow of Storytelling

A few quotes from relevant literature highlight how Futures Literacy and Futures Thinking support and strengthen the capability of both sensing and sense-making.

"This suggests that companies should invest in pedagogically rich scenario processes that develop **the capability of managers to sense changes**. The learning generated by scenario processes can strengthen the 'sensing' dynamic capabilities of firms," is how the academics Martin Rhisiart, Riel Miller and Simon Brooks put it.[99]

"Strategic Foresight positively impacts **sense-making** and learning," academics Sara Moqaddamerad and Murad Ali write, referring to their own research and a handful of other research papers.[100] "Strategic Foresight enriches learning by providing knowledge about an organization's future internal and external environments."

"In the process of becoming futures literate, we become more skilled in imagining and diversifying futures and thus opening ourselves up for emergence, the novelty that is around us," writes the academic Loes Damhof.[101] "**We sense more, but things also make more sense**. This desire to make sense of what we do not know often becomes the source of our agency. When things make sense, we feel more comfortable. When we sense things without making sense of it, we quickly feel uneasy. And in the rush to make sense, we might even fall into the trap of just 'making': doing, acting, making decisions while forgetting to sense anything at all."

Among the leaders and organizations that focus on the future, trends and wanting/needing to adapt, there IS a higher degree of sensing, of organizational consciousness, and of being futures literate. Often unwittingly, these people are attuned to the hidden part of The Iceberg of Culture:

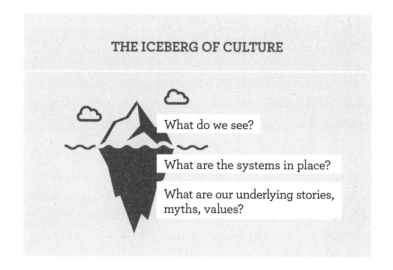

They also (subconsciously, a good deal of the time) spot trends and movements in their field. And they sense internal movements and signals too.

> The correlation between sensing and the practice of Futures Thinking is strong.

These leaders may be **unconsciously competent** regarding sensing, but drawing upon the professional literature (as shown above), Futures Literacy can help them become consciously competent. This, supported by practices of Deep Listening, changes the conditions for change, and as such enables a fundamentally different approach to thinking about the future.

EMOTIONAL IMPACT OF USING THE FUTURES

"It was so amazing to see how the mood in the room changed throughout the day. We started out being sceptical about the transformation, and ended up with hope and taking part in the planning!"
— A Director in a manufacturing company

"Spending time in the imaginary future made it possible to visualize the daily work, the conversations, the tools and software, and our collaboration across the organization. That visualization helped me overcome anxiety about the transformation."
— A Vice President in a life sciences organization

"You know, we can actually do something. It is not all as dark and determined as I thought. Now I know where to use my influence and what scenario I want to cheer for."
— A team lead in a biotech organization

These are examples of the emotional impact that a participatory, action-learning approach to Using the Future can create.

Across the experiences I've had with Futures Thinking processes over the past decade, leading to the creation of this book, a pattern of emotional impact has emerged: four specific, distinct areas of positive psychological principles increase because of the approach.

THE EMOTIONAL IMPACT OF USING THE FUTURE AND ANTICIPATORY LEADERSHIP

The emotional impact

HOCA

Hope

Ownership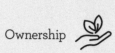

Confidence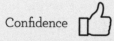

Agency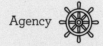

Figure 47
HOCA: The Emotional Impact of Using the Future
and Anticipatory Leadership

Hope for the future.

Ownership of the future and the way forward.

Confidence in the approach.

Agency to act and shape the future.

People express **hope for the future** because they have mentally 'been there,' and experienced the situations through scenarios and detailed descriptions of situations, removing anxiety about the unknown. Jane McGonigal has a wonderful example of this related to simulation of a pandemic prior to COVID-19, when hopeful responses were later sent to her by the participants when the actual pandemic hit in 2020.[102]

They claim **ownership of the scenarios and the transformation** because they have been involved in shaping them, discussing and rethinking the negative assumptions that might discourage them from taking responsibility for both solutions and plans.

They express **confidence in the approach**, as they've been part of analysing the forces and drivers that might affect us. They've sorted the signals that push them, and discussed the myths that hinder them.

Significantly, and most valuable, they recognize that they have **agency to act**. Individual agency, collective agency and agency in the ecosystem. They are not passive spectators, but active creators of the future they want to be a part of. They experience the power of possibilism and start to see the world as being plastic and shapeable.

Entrepreneur Adam Wood[103] has similarly investigated the results of what he calls Future-Minded Leadership, which possess optimism, pragmatism and the ability to envision potential outcomes. His organization, BetterUp Labs, conducted a market survey of 1,500+ US workers and two experimental research studies with 1,000+ participants. They learned that: (a) When individuals effectively tap into future-minded leadership, there are positive shifts in anxiety and depression symptoms; (b) Not only do Future-Minded Leaders report 34% less anxiety and 35% less depression, but they're also more hopeful about the future, more productive, and have greater life satisfaction than those low in Future-Minded Leadership skills. This also has a dramatic effect on team performance, with a double-digit increase in team engagement and risk-taking.

These emotional impacts cannot be ascribed to Futures Thinking methods alone, as noted by researcher Riikka Armanto.[104] The level of genuine involvement and the clarity of mandate and decision-making processes are vital aspects to consider, just as facilitation skills are for workshops.

> # Using the Future has the potential to create hope, ownership, confidence and agency.

We initially observed that many leaders who are responsible for organizational transformations comment on the VUCAness of their business world, and feel the BANIness, in themselves and in their peers and employees. It seems captivating and alluring to engage in Futures Thinking to mitigate these emotions. HOCA — hope, ownership, confidence and agency — might be a potentially mitigating pain reliever against the anxiety we observe in the signals around us.

REFLECTIONS FROM PART FOUR

In this section we investigated the leadership it takes to drive these kinds of Using the Future transformations. We looked at the existing professional literature on futures-ready leadership and compared it to observations on leaders who master Futures Thinking on the inside of the organization.

And with that, we have now answered the four questions that we set out to:

- How do I use my understanding of trends and signals in society and technology to design my organization, culture and governance?
- How do I look for signals inside my organization?
- How do I challenge and revisit our assumptions and myths, which we build our view of the future on?
- What kind of anticipatory leadership does it take to be futures literate inside my organization?

SUMMARY

This chapter focused on discussing Anticipatory Leadership and the emotional impact of Using the Future.

Four capabilities stood out that distinguish leaders who master Anticipatory Leadership on the inside of the organization:

- **Possibilism**: They believe in human agency, not determinism

- **Plasticity**: They believe in adaptation, not rigidity

- **Playfulness**: They approach challenges with joy, creativity and spontaneity

- **Organizational consciousness**: They are aware of both the existing and emerging cultures in the ecosystem, including subcultural, hidden and rebellious movements

The emotional impact of Anticipatory Leadership and Using the Future for transformations:

- **Hope** for the future

- **Ownership** of the future and the way forward

- **Confidence** in the approach

- **Agency** to act and shape the future

TRENDS AND SIGNALS, SENSED AND RECEIVED
BY ERIC SOLOMON

Ph.D., Founder and CEO of The Human OS,
Board Member, Speaker, Author, Coach
Previously, global brand/marketing/strategy positions at
YouTube, Instagram, Spotify

Location: USA

- AI fear and panic. Fear of job replacement, of what jobs will look like. Jobs are changing "from creating to editing."

- Demand for job flexibility. "I want my job to fit my life." Gone is the nine-to-five job, even in New York, notoriously known for lack of work-life balance.

- In-person connections at the office are increasing. "It's more about time than space." Time structure and time shaping are emerging topics. People feel grateful to have a place to go, to feel in-person connections and attend meaningful meetings.

- Investments in people-development are decreasing. "Companies are not teaching people anything anymore." They need to develop themselves, in their own time. People are hired for what they HAVE done, not for their potential.

- The trust barometer for businesses is higher than for other institutions. But will people still trust the businesses? Will more unions pop up?

CONCLUSION

How can we use Futures Thinking as a vehicle for bringing the Future of Work into the context of the inside of our organization?

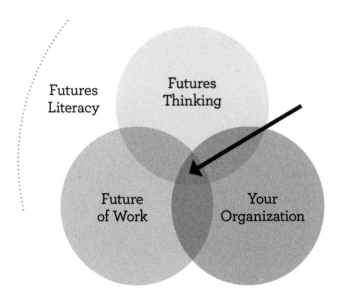

How can we use this knowledge for change management/enablement, and for understanding and designing our transformation?

Throughout this book, several factors have been highlighted as key learning points from using Futures Thinking on the inside of the organization. Eight of these are particularly important when designing your Futures Thinking process:

1. A crucial element that distinguishes Using the Future from a classic strategic process is the explicit and deliberate use of trends and signals for **Signal Sorting** to inform your approach. Paying attention to the shifts and shocks in the ecosystem around you enables you to incorporate them in your tactical transformation, planning and scenarios for change.

2. **Internal Signals** are important to identify, discuss and embrace the subcultural, hidden or rebellious movements in your organization. You can either develop the ability to spot them yourself, make it a habit in your leadership team, or establish a network of Trend Receivers.

3. Working explicitly with the underlying **Anticipatory Assumptions and organizational myths** helps you to reveal them, reframe them and rethink them. They play a role as potential mental blockers or sources of organizational friction. A focused approach to listening, understanding and deconstructing them will increase the quality and credibility of the scenarios.

4. As exemplified via the case studies, **strategizing from the future is a fruitful framing** of the approach to Using the Future. Create the scenarios and make the design of the transformation from the point of view of the future, rather than the present. This will inform your current planning with less ballast from the past, help avoid extrapolating, and instead draw the path backwards from the alternative future.

5. **The futures-ready organization is a Participatory Organization**, with Futures Literacy capabilities and Futures Thinking processes for sensing, exploring, evaluation and sense-making.

6. When shaping the structures, cultures and governance, first **look at updates to the opposite forces, tensions or paradoxes in your organization**. The '5+5 Sliders of opposite forces' is a useful analysis to apply to your scenarios, from which logical conclusions on organizational philosophies, methodologies, design and structures emerge, followed by updates to the business model, governance and cultures.

7. The **Anticipatory Leadership** required for mastering Futures Thinking on the inside of an organization shares many of the capabilities required for Strategic Foresight. However, four traits stand out as critical for Using the Future in the organization: **Possibilism, Plasticity, Playfulness and Organizational consciousness**.

8. The **emotional impact** of properly applied Futures
   Thinking is unambiguous and follows a pattern that
   is recognizable across domains, industries and functions. It creates **Hope, Ownership, Confidence and
   Agency** among the participants.

Two significant pillars underpin our work: Clarity around
the capabilities of Anticipatory Leadership on the inside
of an organization; and the palpable presence of agency in
almost all discussions, models, approaches, requirements,
impacts and effects.

We're talking about agency to act, and to shape the future,
despite apparent obstacles and inherent assumptions.

The belief that the futures are not determined by context and ecosystem, but by human agency, is a significant
trait of Anticipatory Leadership.

Let this be our promise to each other: To strive to connect with our personal and organizational agency, in order
to shape a preferable, desirable, alternative future that we
want to be part of.

Erik Korsvik Østergaard
Summer 2024
The country house Bredemaj,
outside Copenhagen, Denmark

GLOSSARY

Future of Work:
The philosophies, trends and societal/technological movements within work, leadership, culture and organizational design.

New Ways of Working:
When the elements of Future of Work get contextualized and embraced in an organization, New Ways of Working appear. Movements and methodologies like Sociocracy, Agile, Lean Startup and Teal exist in this realm.

Transformation:
A significant and intentional change in the structure, culture, governance, processes or strategies of an organization, as a response to the changing world.

Anticipatory Leadership:
A forward-looking, futures-thinking approach to navigate uncertainty, anticipate emerging trends and signals, and effectively explore and evaluate alternative futures and scenarios, in order to drive the transformation. Anticipatory Leadership is a mindset, methodology and paradigm that uses the future to make decisions about today.

Participatory Organization:
Structures, governance and cultures that enable organizational adaptability, sensing and sense-making, with employee involvement and shared decision-making. A management style that actively involves employees in the exploration and direction-setting process.

Using the Future:
To explore and evaluate future scenarios, in order to make decisions today.

Futures Literacy:
The ability and capacity to think critically and abstractly about the future. Key building blocks are the understanding of anticipation and assumptions.

Futures Thinking:
The creative and investigative process of exploring and evaluating what affects us, to describe scenarios for the futures.

Anticipatory Assumptions:
Expectations or beliefs about future events, scenarios or outcomes that shape and inform our decision-making and our emotional stance toward change.

Trend:
A general direction of change over time, identifiable in societal, technological, economic, environmental and political domains.

Signal:
Concrete, observable evidence in the present that hints at future trends, such as anormal events, new technologies or surprising policies.

Agency:
The capacity to actively shape the future through intentional actions.

RECOMMENDED READING, LISTENING AND WATCHING

Books

Imaginable: How to See the Future Coming and Feel Ready for Anything, Even Things that Seem Impossible Today, by Jane McGonigal.

Strategic Foresight: An Introductory Guide to Practice, by Jan Oliver Schwarz.

SCENARIO reports: Using the Future, by Copenhagen Institute for Futures Studies.

SCENARIO reports: Global Megatrends, by Copenhagen Institute for Futures Studies.

Transforming the Future: Anticipation in the 21st Century, by Riel Miller.

The Future: A Very Short Introduction, by Jennifer M. Gidley.

Strategic Reframing: The Oxford Scenario Planning Approach, by Rafael Ramírez and Angela Wilkinson.

Lead from the Future: How to Turn Visionary Thinking into Breakthrough Growth, by Mark W. Johnson and Josh Suskewicz.

What We Owe the Future: A Million-year View, by William MacAskill.

Strategic Foresight: Learning from the Future, by Patricia Lustig.

Courses

All courses on Futures Thinking by Copenhagen Institute for Future Studies.

The Coursera online courses by Institute for the Future.
The Emergence Academy at Hawkwood Centre for
Future Thinking.

Other online resources to read, subscribe to or follow
Springer Open; subscribe to new articles from
European Journal of Futures Research.
(https://eujournalfuturesresearch.springeropen.com/)
Newsletters from Institute for the Future, Futurism,
Copenhagen Institute for Futures Studies and OECD.
The signal scanning forums at Institute for the Future.
The /r/futurology subreddit at Reddit.
Visit the signal database at Futures Centre.
(https://www.thefuturescentre.org/signals-insights/)
Visit the Foresight Academy.
(https://www.foresightacademy.com/)
Visit the Open Foresight Hub.
(https://openforesighthub.org/)
Visit the Association of Professional Futurists.
(https://www.apf.org/)
Visit the Dubai Future Foundation.
(https://www.dubaifuture.ae/)

Podcasts and videos
A YouTube playlist curated by Wensupu (Wen) Yang, APF.
(https://www.youtube.com/@wenyang4763)
'Future now' podcast by Institute for the Future.
'Fremtidsministeriet' podcast (in Danish) by Copenhagen
Institute for Futures Studies.
'The New Abnormal' podcast hosted by Sean Pillot
de Chenecey.
'Supertrends' podcast (in Danish) by 24syv.

LIST OF FIGURES

ENDNOTES

1. Erik Korsvik Østergaard, 2018. *The Responsive Leader*. LID Publishing.

2. Erik Korsvik Østergaard, 2020. *Teal Dots in an Orange World*. LID Publishing.

3. Riel Miller, 2018. *Transforming the Future: Anticipation in the 21st Century*. UNESCO Publishing.

4. Jan Oliver Schwarz, 2023. *Strategic Foresight: An Introductory Guide to Practice*. Routledge.

5. Mark W Johnson and Josh Suskewicz, 2020. *Lead from the Future: How to Turn Visionary Thinking into Breakthrough Growth*. Harvard Business Review Press.

6. Riel Miller, 2018. *Transforming the Future: Anticipation in the 21st Century*. UNESCO Publishing.

7. Jennifer M. Gidley, 2017. *The Future: A Very Short Introduction*. Oxford University Press.

8. Jamais Cascio. "Facing the Age of Chaos." *medium.com*. https://medium.com/@cascio/facing-the-age-of-chaos-b00687b1f51d

9. John P Kotter. 1995. "Leading Change: Why Transformation Efforts Fail." *Harvard Business Review*. https://hbr.org/1995/05/leading-change-why-transformation-efforts-fail-2.

10. "Losing from Day One: Why Even Successful Transformations Fall Short." *McKinsey*, 2021. https://www.mckinsey.com/capabilities/people-and-organizational-performance/our-insights/successful-transformations

11. John Granger, 2019. "Why Digital Transformation Succeeds. And Why It Doesn't." *ibm.com*. https://www.ibm.com/blog/why-digital-transformation-succeeds-and-why-it-doesnt/.

12. Gary Hamel and Michele Zanini, 2020. *Humanocracy: Creating Organizations as Amazing as the People Inside Them*. Harvard Business Review Press.

13. Good Morning April. 2023. Futures Of Work: Horizon Scanning Document 2023.

14. Jane McGonigal, 2022. *Imaginable: How to See the Future Coming and Feel Ready for Anything: Even Things that Seem Impossible Today.* Spiegel & Grau.

15. Jan Oliver Schwarz, 2023. *Strategic Foresight: An Introductory Guide to Practice.* Routledge.

16. Copenhagen Institute for Futures Studies, 2020. SCENARIO Reports: Using the Future.

17. Riel Miller, 2018. *Transforming the Future: Anticipation in the 21ˢᵗ Century.* UNESCO Publishing.

18. Jennifer M. Gidley, 2017. *The Future: A Very Short Introduction.* Oxford University Press.

19. Copenhagen Institute for Futures Studies, 2020. SCENARIO Reports: Using the Future.

20. René Rohrbeck, Cinzia Battistella and Eelko Huizingh, 2015. "Corporate foresight: An Emerging Field with a Rich Tradition." *Technological Forecasting and Social Change*, December: 1–9.

21. Mark Frauenfelder, 2023. "Five Key Principles for Crafting Engaging and Effective Forecasts." *medium.com*. 25 August. https://medium.com/foresight-matters/five-key-principles-for-crafting-engaging-and-effective-forecasts-287ad6ed3fc2.

22. Adam Gordon, René Rohrbeck and Jan Schwarz, 2019. "Escaping the 'Faster Horses' Trap: Bridging Strategic Foresight and Design-Based Innovation." *Technology Innovation Management Review*, August Volume 9, Issue 8: 30–42.

23. Jan Oliver Schwarz, 2023. *Strategic Foresight: An Introductory Guide to Practice.* Routledge.

24. Good Morning April, 2023. Futures Of Work: Horizon Scanning Document 2023.

25. Marita Canina, Carmen Bruno and Eva Monestier, 2022. "Futures Thinking." *The Palgrave Encyclopedia of the Possible* 1–7.

26. Riel Miller, 2018. *Transforming the Future: Anticipation in the 21ˢᵗ Century.* UNESCO Publishing.

27. Stefan Bergheim, 2023. "Patterns of Anticipatory Assumptions." *ResearchGate.*

28. Jane McGonigal, 2022. *Imaginable: How to See the Future Coming and Feel Ready for Anything: Even Things that Seem Impossible Today.* Spiegel & Grau.

29. Fred Polak, 1973. *The Image of the Future.* Amsterdam, London: Elsevier Scientific Publishing Company.

30. Sohail Inayatullah, 2023. "The Futures Triangle: Origins and Iterations." https://www.researchgate.net/publication/374766163_ The_Futures_Triangle_Origins_and_Iterations

31. Charles W. Taylor, 1990. "Creating Strategic Visions." *Strategic Studies Institute*, U.S. Army War College.

32. Joseph Voros, 2017. "Big History and Anticipation: Using Big History as a Framework for Global Foresight," in R Poli (ed.) *Handbook of Anticipation: Theoretical and Applied Aspects of the Use of Future in Decision Making*. Springer International. https://thevoroscope. com/2017/02/24/the-futures-cone-use-and-history/.

33. Joseph Voros, 2017. "Big History and Anticipation: Using Big History as a Framework for Global Foresight," in R Poli (ed.) *Handbook of Anticipation: Theoretical and Applied Aspects of the Use of Future in Decision Making*. Springer International. Cham. doi:10.1007/978-3-319-31737-3_95-1

34. Copenhagen Institute for Futures Studies, 2020. SCENARIO Reports: Using the Future.

35. Institute for the Future and Sabrina Howard, 2021. "Drivers and Signals: How Are They Different?" 28 June. https://www.iftf.org/insights/drivers-signals-differences/.

36. Nassim Nicholas Taleb, 2007. *The Black Swan: The Impact of the Highly Improbable*. Random House.

37. Rupert Hofmann, 2015. "Visionary Competence for Long-term Development of Brands, Products, and Services: The Trend Receiver Concept and Its First Applications at Audi." *Technological Forecasting and Social Change* 83–98.

38. National Academies of Sciences, Engineering, and Medicine, 2020. *Safeguarding the Bioeconomy*. Washington, DC: The National Academies Press.

39. Jonas Svava Iversen, 2006. "Futures Thinking Methodologies and Options for Education," in *Think Scenarios, Rethink Education*, OECD Publishing.

40. Jan Oliver Schwarz, 2023. *Strategic Foresight: An Introductory Guide to Practice*. Routledge.

41. Riel Miller, 2018. *Transforming the Future: Anticipation in the 21st Century*. UNESCO Publishing.

42. Jerome Glenn, 1972. "Futurizing Teaching vs Futures Course." *Social Science Record*, Syracuse University, Spring Volume IX, No. 3.

43. Stuart Candy and Jake Franklin Dunagan, 2016. "The Experiential Turn." *Human Futures*.

44. Jim Dator, 2009. "Alternative Futures at the Manoa School." *Journal of Futures Studies.*

45. Alun Rhydderch, 2017. "Scenario Building: The 2x2 Matrix Technique." *Futuribles International.*

46. Adrian Müller and Jan Oliver Schwarz, 2016. "Assessing the Functions and Dimensions of Visualizations in Foresight." *Foresight.*

47. Martin Rhisiart, Riel Miller and Simon Brooks, 2014. "Learning to Use the Future: Developing Foresight Capabilities Through Scenario Processes." *Technological Forecasting and Social Change.*

48. Alexander Osterwalder and David J. Bland, 2019. *Testing Business Ideas: A Field Guide for Rapid Experimentation.* Wiley.

49. Copenhagen Institute for Futures Studies, 2020. SCENARIO Reports: Using the Future.

50. Copenhagen Institute for Futures Studies, 2020. SCENARIO Reports: Using the Future.

51. Rafael Popper, 2009. "Foresight Methodology" in *The Handbook of Technology Foresight.* Edward Elgar Publishing.

52. Jan Oliver Schwarz, 2023. *Strategic Foresight: An Introductory Guide to Practice.* Routledge.

53. Riel Miller, 2015. "Learning, the Future, and Complexity: An Essay on the Emergence of Futures Literacy." *European Journal of Education* 50(4), December.

54. Nicklas Larsen, Jeanette Kæseler Mortensen and Riel Miller, 2020. "What Is 'Futures Literacy' and Why Is It Important?" *medium.com.* https://medium.com/copenhagen-institute-for-futures-studies/what-is-futures-literacy-and-why-is-it-important-a27f24b983d8

55. Riel Miller, 2018. *Transforming the Future: Anticipation in the 21st Century.* UNESCO Publishing.

56. Joshua Haiar and South Dakota Public Broadcasting, 2022. "Ethanol's future unclear as electric vehicles grow in popularity." 19 September. https://listen.sdpb.org/business-economics/2022-09-19/ethanols-future-unclear-as-electric-vehicles-grow-in-popularity.

57. Jan Oliver Schwarz, 2023. *Strategic Foresight: An Introductory Guide to Practice.* Routledge.

58. Stefan Bergheim, 2023. "Patterns of Anticipatory Assumptions." *ResearchGate.*

59. Good Morning April. 2023. Futures Of Work: Horizon Scanning Document 2023.

60. Jan Oliver Schwarz, 2023. *Strategic Foresight: An Introductory Guide to Practice*. Routledge.

61. Riel Miller, 2018. *Transforming the Future: Anticipation in the 21st Century*. UNESCO Publishing.

62. C. Otto Scharmer, 2009. *Theory U: Leading from the Future as It Emerges*. Berrett-Koehler Publishers.

63. Joseph Voros, 2017. "Big History and Anticipation: Using Big History as a Framework for Global Foresight," in R Poli (ed.) *Handbook of Anticipation: Theoretical and Applied Aspects of the Use of Future in Decision Making*. Springer International. https://thevoroscope.com/2017/02/24/the-futures-cone-use-and-history/.

64. Martin Rhisiart, Riel Miller and Simon Brooks, 2014. "Learning to Use the Future: Developing Foresight Capabilities Through Scenario Processes." *Technological Forecasting and Social Change*.

65. Jan Oliver Schwarz, 2023. *Strategic Foresight: An Introductory Guide to Practice*. Routledge.

66. Jan Oliver Schwarz and Gerhard Schönhofer, 2024. "Using AI for Developing Foresight: Reflections on an Experiment." https://www.linkedin.com/pulse/using-ai-developing-foresight-reflections-experiment-schwarz-gpikf.

67. Eric Ries, 2011. *The Lean Startup: How Today's Entrepreneurs Use Continuous Innovation to Create Radically Successful Business.* Crown Currency.

68. Alexander Osterwalder and David J. Bland, 2019. *Testing Business Ideas: A Field Guide for Rapid Experimentation.* Wiley.

69. Rupert Hofmann, 2015. "Visionary Competence for Long-term Development of Brands, Products, and Services: The Trend Receiver Concept and Its First Applications at Audi." *Technological Forecasting and Social Change* 83–98.

70. Jane McGonigal, 2022. *Imaginable: How to See the Future Coming and Feel Ready for Anything: Even Things that Seem Impossible Today.* Spiegel & Grau.

71. Otti Vogt, 2024. *linkedin.com*. https://www.linkedin.com/posts/ottivogt_beyondindividualism-organizationaldynamics-activity-7163826767084920832-GrwN/.

72. Norbert Weiner, 1948. *Cybernetics: Or Control and Communication in the Animal and the Machine*. The MIT Press.

73. Riel Miller, 2018. *Transforming the Future: Anticipation in the 21st Century*. UNESCO Publishing.

74. Stefan Bergheim, 2023. "Patterns of Anticipatory Assumptions." *ResearchGate*.

75. Aaron Dignan, 2019. *Brave New Work: Are You Ready to Reinvent Your Organization?* Portfolio.

76. Gustavo Razzetti, 2019. "How to Use the Culture Design Canvas: A Culture Mapping Tool." *www.fearlessculture.design*.

77. Strategyzer, 2024. "The Business Model Canvas." https://www.strategyzer.com/library/the-business-model-canvas.

78. Strategyzer, 2024. "The Value Proposition Canvas." https://www.strategyzer.com/library/the-value-proposition-canvas.

79. Mark Richman, 2014. Alignment vs. Autonomy. https://markrichman.com/alignment-vs-autonomy/.

80. Stanley McChrystal, Tantum Collins, David Silverman and Chris Fussell, 2015. *Team of Teams: New Rules of Engagement for a Complex World*. Portfolio.

81. Erik Korsvik Østergaard, 2020. *Teal Dots in an Orange World*. London: LID Publishing

82. Responsive Org.: Responsive Manifesto. https://www.responsive.org/manifesto

83. Erik Korsvik Østergaard, 2020. *Teal Dots in an Orange World*. London: LID Publishing.

84. Ted J. Rau and Jerry Koch-Gonzalez, 2018. *Many Voices One Song: Shared Power with Sociocracy*. Sociocracy For All.

85. Jeff Sutherland and J. J. Sutherland. 2014. *Scrum: The Art of Doing Twice the Work in Half the Time*, Crown Currency.

86. Eric Ries, 2011. *The Lean Startup: How Today's Entrepreneurs Use Continuous Innovation to Create Radically Successful Business*. Crown Currency.

87. Frederic Laloux, 2014. *Reinventing Organizations: A Guide to Creating Organizations Inspired by the Next Stage in Human Consciousness*. Nelson Parker.

88. Deloitte, 2017. "Rewriting the Rules for the Digital Age: 2017 Deloitte Global Human Capital Trends." Deloitte.

89. Wouter Aghina, Karin Ahlback, Aaron De Smet, Gerald Lackey, Michael Lurie, Monica Murarka and Christopher Handscomb, 2018. "The Five Trademarks of Agile Organizations." *McKinsey.com*.

90. Stanley McChrystal, Tantum Collins, David Silverman and Chris Fussell, 2015. *Team of Teams: New Rules of Engagement for a Complex World*. Portfolio.

91. Wei-Xing Zhou, Didier Sornette, Russell Hill and Robin Dunbar, 2005. "Discrete Hierarchical Organization of Social Group Sizes." Proceedings of the Royal Society B 439–444.

92. Good Morning April. 2023. Futures Of Work: Horizon Scanning Document 2023.

93. Michael Sales and Anika Savage, 2008. "The Anticipatory Leader: Futurist, Strategist and Integrator." *Strategy and Leadership*, November.

94. Adam Wood, 2022. "Meet the Future-Minded Leader: Your Organization's Answer to Uncertainty." *Betterup.com*. 11 January. https://www.betterup.com/blog/insights-report-future-minded-leader.

95. Marina Gorbis, 2019. "Five Principles for Thinking Like a Futurist." 11 March. https://er.educause.edu/articles/2019/3/five-principles-for-thinking-like-a-futurist.

96. Melissa Innes, 2023. "Exploring the Lived Experience of Individual Foresight in Organisations." Thesis, University of the Sunshine Coast, Queensland.

97. Jan Oliver Schwarz, 2023. *Strategic Foresight: An Introductory Guide to Practice*. Routledge.

98. David Rome, 2010. Deep Listening. https://www.mindful.org/deep-listening/.

99. Martin Rhisiart, Riel Miller and Simon Brooks, 2014. "Learning to Use the Future: Developing Foresight Capabilities Through Scenario Processes." *Technological Forecasting and Social Change.*

100. Sara Moqaddamerad and Murad Ali, 2024. "Strategic Foresight and Business Model Innovation: The Sequential Mediating Role of Sensemaking and Learning." *Technological Forecasting and Social Change,* Volume 200.

101. Loes Damhof, 2021. "Sensing and Sense Making: Why We Need the Ways of the Trickster to Truly Embrace Uncertainty." *medium.com*. 20 February. https://loesdamhof.medium.com/sensing-and-sense-making-a12b43ce0762.

102. Jane McGonigal, 2022. *Imaginable: How to See the Future Coming and Feel Ready for Anything: Even Things that Seem Impossible Today*. Spiegel & Grau.

103. Adam Wood, 2022. "Meet the Future-Minded Leader: Your Organization's Answer to Uncertainty." *Betterup.com*. 11 January. https://www.betterup.com/blog/insights-report-future-minded-leader.

104. Anna Riikka Airiina Armanto, 2024. "Futures Participation as Anticipatory Practice — What do Futures Workshops Do?" *European Journal of Futures Research.*

AN INTRODUCTION TO
ERIK KORSVIK ØSTERGAARD

Erik Korsvik Østergaard (b. 1973) is a futures thinker, leadership advisor, speaker and author. Some people call him a 'CEO Whisperer,' alluding to his role as an organizational advisor at the C-suite level.

With a background in engineering (MSc in Applied Mathematics), Erik has held numerous leadership roles as project manager, program manager and people manager in large, complex, regulated industries. For the past decade, he has been self-employed, helping leaders in scale-ups, SMBs and corporate enterprises understand the Future of Work and embrace their own New Ways of Working. He is a popular speaker and advisor, helping organizations in many countries and with numerous cultural backgrounds, but with a preference for large, complex, regulated industries.

He has previously written two books on progressive leadership and organizational design. The first, *The Responsive Leader*, was published in 2018 and described the roles and behaviours of progressive, modern leaders. The follow-up, *Teal Dots in an Orange World*, came out in 2020 and focused on the organizational design of pockets of progressiveness inside classic, hierarchical organizations, inspired by the work of organizational reinvention advisor and coach Frederic Laloux.

This book, *Anticipatory Leadership*, is a continuation of Erik's focus on the future of work, leadership and culture. It will bring Futures Literacy, Futures Thinking and Strategic Foresight into play in the tactical world of organizational change management — on the inside of your organization.